# PRIORITIES
## *in* PRACTICE

# The Essentials of Mathematics K–6

## Effective Curriculum, Instruction, and Assessment

## Kathy Checkley

Association for Supervision and Curriculum Development • Alexandria, Virginia USA

Association for Supervision and Curriculum Development
1703 N. Beauregard St. • Alexandria, VA 22311-1714 USA
Telephone: 1-800-933-2723 or 1-703-578-9600 • Fax: 1-703-575-5400
Web site: www.ascd.org • E-mail: member@ascd.org

Kathy Checkley is a writer and project manager at ASCD. She has been a journalist for more than 25 years and has spent the past 12 years focusing on issues in education.

Gene R. Carter, *Executive Director*; Michelle Terry, *Deputy Executive Director, Program Development*; Nancy Modrak, *Director of Publishing*; Julie Houtz, *Director of Book Publishing*; John Wilcox, *Director of Newsletters and Special Publications*; John Franklin, *Project Manager*; Kathy Checkley, *Author*; Mary Beth Nielsen, *Manager, Editorial Services*; Lisa Post, *Associate Editor*; Gary Bloom, *Director, Design and Production Services*; Georgia Park, *Senior Designer*; Keith Demmons, *Typesetter*; Vivian Coss, *Production Specialist*

All Web links, names, addresses, and other information in this book are correct as of the publication date. If you notice a deactivated or changed Web link, please e-mail books@ascd.org with the words "Link Update" in the subject line. In your message, please specify the Web link, the book title, and the page number on which the link appears.

ASCD is committed to diversity and encourages educators from diverse backgrounds to contact the Association for consideration regarding possible publishing opportunities and collaborations.

Printed in the United States of America.

2006 sale book. ASCD Premium, Comprehensive, and Regular members periodically receive ASCD books as part of their membership benefits.

ISBN-13: 978-1-4166-0369-6  ISBN-10: 1-4166-0369-7

ASCD product #106032

ASCD member price: $18.95     nonmember price: $23.95

**Library of Congress Cataloging-in-Publication Data**

Checkley, Kathy.
  The essentials of mathematics, K–6 : effective curriculum, instruction, and assessment / Kathy Checkley.
     p. cm. -- (Priorities in practice)
  Includes bibliographical references and index.
  ISBN-13: 978-1-4166-0369-6 (pbk. : alk. paper)
  ISBN-10: 1-4166-0369-7 (pbk. : alk. paper)  1. Mathematics--Study and teaching (Elementary)--United States. 2. Mathematics--Study and teaching (Middle school)--United States. I. Title. II. Series.

  QA135.6.C5253 2006
  372.7--dc22
                        2005037868

13 12 11 10 09 08 07 06          1 2 3 4 5 6 7 8 9 10 11 12 13

# PRIORITIES *in* PRACTICE
# The Essentials of Mathematics, K–6

# Acknowledgments

Many thanks! This book could not have been written without the kindness, patience, and generosity of all the teachers and educators interviewed.

Special thanks go to Beth Peters, who supplied several of the classroom photos and samples of student work that appear in the book, and to Leanne Luttrell and Cynthia Cliche who also supplied samples of student work.

Special thanks also go to

- Leanne Luttrell for pouring over the initial draft of this book and pointing out any errors or misconceptions.

- Cathy Seeley, who was always willing to take a few minutes to help clarify thinking.

- John Franklin, for his tireless efforts to keep this project on track—and for issuing the challenge to stretch just a little bit more.

At the time the book was being written, educators interviewed could be reached at the following locations:

Ashley Berk, Travell Elementary School, Ridgewood, New Jersey

Jim Bohan, Mainheim Township School District, Lancaster, Pennsylvania

Jennifer Buttars, Columbia Elementary School, West Jordan, Utah

Thomas P. Carpenter, University of Wisconsin–Madison

LeeAnn Cervini, Terry A. Taylor Elementary School, Spencerport, New York

Cynthia Cliche, Homer Pittard Campus School, Murfreesboro, Tennessee

Linda Figgins, McKinley Elementary School, Elgin, Illinois

Cindy Hansford, Meadow View Elementary School, Helena, Alabama

John Holloway, Educational Testing Service, Princeton, New Jersey

Leanne Luttrell, Sycamore Elementary School, Sugar Hill, Georgia

Matthew Perini, Silver Strong & Associates, Ho-Ho-Kus, New Jersey

Beth Peters, Village East Elementary, Aurora, Colorado

Francine Plotycia, Abingdon Elementary School, Maryland

Barbara J. Reys, University of Missouri, Columbia

Valerie Rose-Piver, Hillview Crest Elementary School, Hayward, California

Mark Saul, National Science Foundation, Arlington, Virginia

Cathy Seeley, National Council of Teachers of Mathematics, Reston, Virginia

Mary Short, Long Neck Elementary School, Millsboro, Delaware

Harvey F. Silver, Silver Strong & Associates, Ho-Ho-Kus, New Jersey

Gail Underwood, Grant Elementary School, Columbia, Missouri

John Van de Walle, Virginia Commonwealth University,
   Richmond

**Author's note:** The teachers featured in this publication each received a 2004 Presidential Award for Excellence in Mathematics and Science Teaching.

# Introduction

*Math is like love—a simple idea, but it can get complicated.*

—Anonymous

*Is it important that students learn mathematics?*

Anyone answer no? It's unlikely. Indeed, mathematics has always had a guaranteed spot in the K–12 curriculum, unlike some of its step-sibling content areas, such as physical education, music, and art.

Pose a slightly different question, however, and the answer may not be so quick or definitive:

*Is learning mathematics a cultural imperative?*

Before you answer yes, consider what happens when mathematics knowledge—or lack thereof—is put to the test:

You're at a party and, with an apologetic laugh, you admit that the ability to do math is beyond you—in fact, you have a hard time even balancing your checkbook! Among the crowd, one or two people may nod in sympathetic understanding.

Now, imagine that, at that same party, you instead confess that you can't read or write.

The reaction, says Thomas Armstrong, would be quite different. He uses this scenario to underscore the importance placed on literacy in the United States. "Not to be able to read in our culture is a source of shame and humiliation for many," he writes in *Multiple Intelligences of Reading and Writing: Making the Words Come Alive* (2003, p. 5).

Does mathematical illiteracy produce the same disquiet? It's often *said* that a sound mathematics education is key to success in life, but a prevailing ambivalence about whether all students need to become skilled in the subject may suggest otherwise.

"For no other subject in the school curriculum is an adult so proud of having done poorly; failure in mathematics is almost a badge of honor," writes Alfred S. Posamentier in "Marvelous Math!" (2004, p. 44). Posamentier, the dean of the school of education at City College of New York, notes that too many adults "seldom remember math class" as a place where they experienced "learning highs."

Do parents want their children to learn math? When asked, most parents will always answer yes, says Barbara J. Reys, distinguished professor of mathematics education at the University of Missouri. She adds, however, that some parents will say, "I wasn't good at math"; some parents also believe that not all students can learn mathematics and that "if they don't, it's okay," says Reys.

This vacillation may stem from parents' own unfavorable experiences with math in school, states Reys. It can also result from another kind of angst: Unlike with reading, "it's not too long before kids are studying math that's beyond what their parents studied. Parents are [then] out of the picture," she observes. Educators, too, have communicated mixed signals about how necessary it is for all students to learn mathematics, especially upper-level subjects like

---

## What Is Mathematical Literacy?

To be literate in mathematics means that one possesses procedural and computational skills, as well as a conceptual understanding of mathematical concepts.

Mathematical literacy today means mastering the "traditional" basics—achieving computational fluency—and attaining a basic understanding of algebra, geometry, measurement, and data analysis and probability.

*Source:* Adapted from *Administrator's Guide: How to Support and Improve Mathematics Education in Your School* (pp. 3, 28), by A. J. Mirra, 2003, Reston, VA: National Council of Teachers of Mathematics.

algebra and calculus. "Until recently, many people thought about mathematics as a discipline that is comprehensible to only a select, talented few," write Lynn T. Goldsmith and Ilene Kantrov in *Guiding Curriculum Decisions for Middle-Grades Mathematics*. "Instructional traditions paid little attention to helping students make sense of the mathematical ideas they encountered," the authors state (2001, p. 37).

Researcher John H. Holloway agrees, adding that there has also been an instructional tradition of holding minority students to lower expectations. "Minority students as a group experience a less rigorous curriculum," which leads to fewer opportunities to succeed in "gateway courses," such as Algebra 1, he writes in "Research Link: Closing the Achievement Gap in Math" (2004, p. 84).

## Slow, But Steady, Change

The societal acceptance of poor mathematics achievement is waning. Dissatisfaction with poor math performance has "become intense and it is growing," write the authors of *Mathematical Proficiency for All Students*. "Every student now needs competency in mathematics," the RAND Mathematics Study Panel asserts. To become mathematically competent, students need to acquire specific knowledge, skills, abilities, and beliefs.

According to researchers at the National Research Council, there are five aspects of mathematical knowledge—five strands—that children must develop throughout their elementary school and middle school years. The five strands, described in *Helping Children Learn Mathematics* (2002, National Academy Press), are interwoven and interdependent. They are

• **Understanding:** This involves comprehending mathematical concepts, operations, and relations, as well as knowing what mathematical symbols, diagrams, and procedures mean. When students have a sound grasp of fundamental mathematical ideas, they know more than isolated facts and procedures. Students know why a mathematical idea is important and when a particular concept is useful. When students truly understand, they are aware of the many connections between mathematical ideas.

• **Computing:** This includes being able to accurately use, with ease, procedures for adding, subtracting, multiplying, and dividing mentally or with paper and pencil. It also involves knowing when and how to use these procedures appropriately. Additionally, the National Research Council broadened its definition of computing from its original meaning—the ability to do arithmetic—to its new definition—the ability to use other mathematical procedures, such as measuring lengths, solving algebraic equations, constructing similar geometric figures, and interpreting and graphing data, like statistics.

• **Applying:** A concept or procedure is not useful unless students recognize when and where to use it—as well as when and where it does not apply. Outside school, students encounter real-life situations and must determine what kind of problem is inherent in each situation. Students, therefore, must be able to discern problems, devise solution strategies, and choose the most useful of those strategies. What's more, students must develop an ability to estimate quantities in their minds or draw them on paper, and they need to know how to distinguish what is known and relevant from what is unknown and irrelevant.

• **Reasoning:** Reasoning is the glue that holds mathematics together. By thinking about the logical relationships between concepts and situations, students can navigate through the elements of a problem and see how they fit together.

• **Engaging:** Engaging in mathematical activity is the key to success. Students should embrace the idea that mathematics makes sense and that—given reasonable effort—they can learn it and use it, both in school and outside school. (Kilpatrick & Swafford, 2002)

*"Standards . . . have helped validate the importance of math."*
—Jim Bohan,
A Standards Primer

Mathematically proficient students know that math is sensible, useful, and worthwhile—and they know that their efforts to learn it will pay off. When students are engaged in mathematics, they know they are effective learners, doers, and users of mathematics. "This goal of achieving mathematical proficiency for all students is unprecedented" (RAND, 2003, p. 2).

A new consciousness about the importance of math has started to "bubble up," notes Cathy Seeley, president of the National Council of Teachers of Mathematics (NCTM). She credits educators' knowledge of the achievement gap, the rise in technology, and "an inundation of information that comes in a statistical and quantitative form," as some of the main factors in helping to shift attitudes.

Jim Bohan credits the standards movement, which NCTM helped to spur, for the increased focus on improving achievement in math (*see A Standards Primer, p. 8*). Bohan is the K–12 mathematics program coordinator in the Mainheim Township School District in Lancaster, Penn. "There are tests now," and there's

# A Standards Primer

When the National Council of Teachers of Mathematics (NCTM) published a series of standards documents in 1989, the council signaled "shifts in emphasis" in math education in curriculum, instruction, and assessment, writes Jim Bohan in *Mathematics: A Chapter of the Curriculum Handbook* (2002):

- Curriculum would emphasize a deeper study of mathematical ideas and concepts and how they are applied today.

- Learning would become more active, students would become more involved with mathematics, and all students would be given opportunities to reach their mathematical potential.

- Student achievement would be assessed through many sources of evidence. (p. 1)

Many educators and professionals accepted the standards, but "resistance to both the vision and implementation of the NCTM standards became substantial and well-organized," Bohan writes (2002, p. 1).

In response to this opposition—as well as to "changes in society, and to the greater understanding of children and learning" (Bohan, 2002, p. 1)—NCTM published the *Principles and Standards for School Mathematics*. Released in 2000, the new standards are intended to be a resource to mathematics curriculum planners, Bohan explains.

According to Bohan, the NCTM standards can help educators develop a mathematics education program that helps students acquire skills and processes that go beyond "computational or symbolic manipulating prowess." That kind of program meets business and industrial expectations of school mathematics. As early as 1987, Bohan writes, Bell Laboratories mathematician Henry Pollack indicated that students should graduate from school with

- The ability to set up problems with appropriate operations.

- A knowledge of a variety of techniques to approach and work on problems.

- An understanding of the underlying mathematical features of a problem.

- The ability to work with others on problems.

- The ability to see the applicability of mathematical ideas to common and complex problems.

- A skill for working with messy problem situations because most real problems are not well formulated.

- The belief in the utility and value of mathematics. (Bohan, 2002, p. 3)

A standards-based mathematics program can help students attain these skills, Bohan maintains. "In many places in the United States, the move to a standards-based math program has produced students who are indeed empowered with the mathematical knowledge to meet any challenge in the future" (2002, p. 4).

*Source:* Adapted from Mathematics: *A Chapter of the Curriculum Handbook* (pp. 1–4), by J. Bohan, 2002, Alexandria, VA: Association for Supervision and Curriculum Development.

accountability. The importance of math, Bohan says, has been validated. And none too soon, many educators assert.

The results of international studies released in December 2004 suggest that mathematics education reform in the United States has been successful on some fronts, but disappointing on others. One such success: 8th grade students who participated in the Trends in International Mathematics and Sciences Study (TIMSS) scored better in both math and science then they had previously. One disappointment: the scores of 15-year-olds who took the Program for International Student Assessment (PISA) were below average in mathematics literacy and problem solving (Association for Supervision and Curriculum Development, 2004/2005).

Perhaps even more important than performance on international tests is the fact that education and career opportunities, as well monetary success, are directly linked to mathematics achievement. The research shows that

• Students who completed higher-level mathematics courses in high school were more likely to earn a bachelor's degree. A longitudinal study conducted by Clifford Adelman, a senior research analyst for the U.S. Department of Education, found that eight percent of high school graduates with algebra 1 under their belts earned a bachelor's degree by age 30. In contrast, 80 percent of those who completed calculus in high school earned a bachelor's degree by age 30 (Adelman, 1999).

• More than half the workers earning more than $40,000 a year had completed two or more credits at the Algebra 2 level or higher. This is according to Anthony P. Carnevale and Donna M. Desrochers of the Educational Testing Service, who analyzed data from the National Educational Longitudinal Survey (Carnevale & Desrochers, 2002).

• Taking higher-level math courses can boost a young person's earning potential after high school, Heather Rose and Julian R. Betts report in *Math Matters: The Links Between High School Curriculum, College Graduation, and Earnings*. Rose and Betts, of the Public Policy Institute of California, found that after controlling for students' demographic, family, and high school characteristics, one extra course in algebra or geometry is associated with 6.3 percent higher earnings (Rose & Betts, 2001).

"Math opens up career paths, empowers consumers, makes meaningful all kinds of data, from basketball statistics to political polls to the latest trends in the stock market," write Harvey F. Silver and Richard W. Strong in the forward to *Styles and Strategies for Teaching Middle School Mathematics* (Silver & Strong, 2003, p. 5). For all these positive outcomes, however, Silver and Strong note a troubling reality: the longer a majority of students are in school, the less they trust in their ability to do math. The authors point out that more than three quarters of all students who graduate from high school don't believe that they are among the "special realm" of people who can be successful in a field that requires in-depth mathematics knowledge.

And that's a serious problem. "If we send an army of math-haters out into today's competitive global culture, we are short-changing millions of students by severely limiting their chances of future success," warn Silver and Strong (2003, p. 5). One response, therefore, would be to create an army of math-lovers—among students, teachers, administrators, and parents. The question is how.

That's the reason for this book—to showcase effective curriculum, instruction, and assessment in mathematics. In doing so, we will

- Give teachers ideas for instructional and assessment approaches that they will want to enthusiastically adopt.

- Share examples of curricula that can inspire a love of mathematics among children and young adults.

- Give administrators ideas for creating a school climate that supports high mathematics achievement for all students.

We will also share examples of professional development that is effective in helping build and enhance our teachers' knowledge of the mathematics they teach.

"The importance of mathematical literacy and the need to understand and use mathematics in everyday life and in the workplace has never been greater and will continue to increase," writes Amy J. Mirra in *Administrator's Guide: How to Support and Improve Mathematics Education in Your School* (2003, p. 1). We hope this book will help educators address the challenge of providing a sound mathematics education for all students. It's nothing short of imperative.

# Trends in Mathematics

*Mathematics, in its widest significance,*
*is the development of all types of formal,*
*necessary, deductive reasoning.*

—*Alfred North Whitehead,*
A Treatise on Universal Algebra

It wasn't easy to be a pioneering U.S. math teacher in the days before the National Council of Teachers of Mathematics (NCTM) released the *Curriculum and Evaluation Standards for School Mathematics*. Just ask Mark Saul, an award-winning teacher who spent more than 30 years working with a wide range of students from the 3rd through the 12th grades. Pushing the envelope was discouraged, he recalls; innovators, rebuked. If a teacher taught math in a traditional way and it "didn't work"—if students didn't understand the content—colleagues were sympathetic. "They would say, 'Oh, you had a bad lot,'" Saul explains. If a teacher got the same result after trying something extra or different, however, colleagues were less generous. The response then became, "It's your fault."

## Emphasizing Algebraic Thinking, Problem Solving, and Communication

Fortunately, with the release of the NCTM standards in 1989, what was once radical became standard, says Saul, who also served as a program officer at the National Science Foundation. The standards-based approach to mathematics education legitimized his routinely going outside the box to help students see how great mathematics could be.

Nearly two decades and one revision later, the standards (now entitled *Principles and Standards for School Mathematics*) continue to support and inspire the practice of radical educators, like Saul. Their staying power underscores the need for a shared, national understanding of the math content that should be emphasized, pre-K through 12th grade, along with the processes and attitudes children should attain.

Articulation across the grades is a big concern in mathematics education today, Saul affirms. The NCTM standards, he notes, outline the broad areas of mathematical knowledge that students should, ideally, build over time and grade levels. Achievement in algebra in high school, therefore, depends on students learning to think algebraically in earlier grades. Likewise, U.S. students will fare better on international exams that emphasize problem solving if they learn, even as early as kindergarten, how to pull problems apart and identify the essence of those problems.

"Nearly all other countries, especially those that outperform the United States in mathematics, have a continuous math program from elementary through secondary school," observed Cathy Seeley, president of NCTM, during an online chat with educators from around the world (Seeley, 2005, para. 18). "I like the idea of introducing algebraic ideas in the elementary grades and in middle school," she continued (2005, para. 42).

*Algebra is something that you [can] start as soon as you enter school.*
—Cathy Seeley
Algebra, K–12

## Thinking Algebraically

That Seeley likes the idea of introducing algebra in the early grades is somewhat an understatement. Emphasizing algebraic thinking in the early grades was the professional development focus for NCTM in 2004–05. The rationale for the emphasis was clear, according to Seeley: too many U.S. high school students struggle with algebra.

# Algebra, K–12

### By Cathy Seeley

Developing algebraic thinking is a process, not an event. Algebraic thinking includes recognizing and analyzing patterns, studying and representing relationships, making generalizations, and analyzing how things change.

At the earliest grades, young children work with patterns. At an early age, children have a natural love of mathematics, and their curiosity is a strong motivator as they try to describe and extend patterns of shapes, colors, sounds, and, eventually, letters and numbers. And at a young age, children can begin to make generalizations about patterns that seem to be the same or different. This kind of categorizing and generalizing is an important developmental step on the journey toward algebraic thinking.

Throughout the elementary grades, patterns are not only an object of study but a tool as well. As students develop their understanding of numbers, they can use patterns in arrays of dots or objects to help them recognize what 6 is or whether 2 is larger than 3. As they explore and understand addition, subtraction, multiplication, and division, they can look for patterns that help them learn procedures and facts. Patterns in rows and columns of objects help students get a sense of multiplication and see that facts make sense. Patterns within the multiplication table itself are interesting to children and help them both learn their facts and understand relationships among those facts. The process of noticing and exploring patterns sets the stage for looking at more complex relationships, including proportionality, in later grades.

As students move into the middle grades, their mathematics experience can focus on connecting their work with numbers and operations to more symbolic work with equations and expressions. At this level, the focus of the mathematics program should be on proportionality—perhaps the most important connecting idea in the entire preK–12 mathematics curriculum. This concept should take students well beyond the study of ratios, proportions, and percent. A real understanding of proportionality allows students to connect their experience with numbers and operations to ideas that they have studied in geometry, measurement, and data analysis. They begin to get a sense of how two quantities can be related proportionally, as seen on maps, scale drawings, and similar figures, or in calculating sales tax or commissions.

A solid understanding of proportionality sets the stage for students to succeed in the more formal study of algebra. From this base, notions of linearity and linear functions emerge naturally. As students explore how to use linear functions to solve problems, the bigger world of functions that may not be linear begins to open for them. Looking at what is the same and what is different among functions lies at the heart of understanding algebraic skills and processes.

*Source:* Adapted with permission from "A Journey in Algebraic Thinking," by C. Seeley, 2004. Retrieved May 16, 2005, from www.nctm.org/news/president/2004_09president.htm

For a long time, she says, there was a "very strong numerical focus in K–8." Students then had to make a giant leap into algebra, but it doesn't have to be that way, Seeley asserts. "Algebra is something that you [can] start as soon as you enter school."

It's not teaching algebra, per se, notes Thomas P. Carpenter, emeritus professor of curriculum and instruction at the University of Wisconsin–Madison. "We're not saying 'Let's go down and teach kids how to solve equations,'" he says. Instead, it involves helping children recognize patterns and teaching arithmetic in ways that are more consistent with how it is used in formal algebra.

For example, teachers may ask a child to solve this equation: $10 + 2 = \_\_$ by asking, "What is 10 plus 2?" If the teacher never points out that the equal sign means *the same as*, students may mistakenly come to think that the equal sign merely signals that they have to perform some kind of operation. A slight shift in language, "What is 10 plus 2 the same as?" can help students build a deeper understanding of equivalence (Carpenter & Romberg, 2004, p. 39; *see Resource Review: All About the Equal Sign, p. 20*).

When armed with the correct meaning of the equal sign, students are better equipped to see how numbers and symbols can be interchangeable in mathematical equations. Students can start substituting variables for numbers much earlier than traditionally thought, Carpenter says. And, if students learn these fundamental ideas early, "there's not so great a transition when algebra [the subject] comes."

*A slight shift in language can help students deepen understanding of equivalence.*

If introducing algebraic concepts earlier in a child's schooling helps make the move to the subject more seamless, then it's reasonable to expect that more children will achieve in algebra. And that, says Robert P. Moses, is important for two reasons. One reason is equity. "Algebra is a gatekeeper subject," he told *Educational Leadership*. "Too many poor children and children of color are denied access to upper-level math classes—to full citizenship, really—because they don't know algebra," states Moses (Checkley, 2001, p. 6), who founded the Algebra Project, a national mathematics literacy effort aimed at helping low-income students and students of color achieve higher-level mathematical skills.

A second reason to introduce algebra early is because of technology and the careers it spawns. For students to get a job

## Resource Review: All About the Equal Sign

Helping students develop a deep understanding of what "equal" means is the subject of a featured lesson in *Powerful Practices in Mathematics and Science,* a multimedia resource based on the research of the National Center for Improving Student Learning and Achievement in Mathematics and Science (NCISLA).

In the lesson for grade 4, which was videotaped for one of the two CD-ROMs included in the resource, the teacher writes this number sentence on the board:

$8 + 4 = \underline{\phantom{xx}} + 5$

Students initially believe that the number 12 will make the number sentence true.

Recognizing that her students hold a common misconception that the equal sign symbols an operation, the teacher helps students come to see why 12 can't be right. She doesn't immediately correct the students; instead, she uses the incorrect response as an entry point into a lesson about equivalence.

First, the teacher poses number sentences in nonstandard forms:

$7 = 3 + 4$ and $6 = 6 + 0$

Then, the teacher challenges students to determine whether these equations are true or false. Working together to discuss the problems, children come to see that the equal sign signifies balance. As the teacher works with groups of students, she gradually introduces the language that will guide students in their discussions. For example, she uses phrases like "is the same as" to convey the correct meaning of the equal sign.

When all the students are ready, the teacher asks them to share their strategies and explain their reasoning. She does not tell students if an answer is wrong but gives other examples and asks questions that enable students to ultimately figure out what works mathematically.

The lesson on the equal sign is one example of many included in *Powerful Practices* that helps illustrate an NCISLA-approved approach to teaching mathematics and science. Thomas P. Carpenter, emeritus professor at the University of Wisconsin and a coauthor of the materials, says the program is designed to focus on how mathematicians and scientists approach unknowns, to highlight and "demystify" the practices they follow to "come up with explanations for the underlying causes of things."

The three practices that mathematicians and scientists engage in—and that students can, too—are constructing models, making generalizations, and justifying those generalizations. "These are sense-making activities," says Carpenter. "Mathematics and science becomes easier to learn when it's done this way. The content sticks."

---

*Source:* Adapted from *Powerful Practices in Mathematics and Science* (pp. 1, 39), by P. T. Carpenter and T. A. Romberg, 2004, Madison, WI: The Board of Regents, University of Wisconsin System. The program is distributed by Learning Point Associates. Order copies of Powerful Practices online at mscproducts@contact.learningpt.org.

and support a family in a world "driven by technology," students need a new literacy, Moses asserted. "Computers are run by symbolic systems. To understand the language of computers, we must have an understanding of a mathematics that encodes quantitative data and creates symbolic representations. The place in the curriculum where students are introduced to such a language is algebra" (Checkley, 2001, p. 6).

## Solving Problems, Developing Reasoning

The attention to strengthening students' algebraic thinking in the early grades is matched by an effort to help students hone their problem-solving skills—an area that's ripe for improvement, given how U.S. students fared on the Program for International Students Assessment (PISA) in 2004.

Reform-minded educators want to be sure that the mathematics curricula allow students to grapple with the myriad of problems they will eventually encounter, says Barbara J. Reys, distinguished professor of mathematics at the University of Missouri. Children must learn the skills of mathematics, but they must also learn to use those skills to "reduce a complex situation into something they can represent and sort out," she says. Children are "presented with lots of numerical information," observes Reys. "The more comfortable they are in analyzing that data, the better the decisions they'll make."

The ability to problem solve is a tremendous life skill that has a much broader application than school mathematics, says NCTM's Seeley. In learning to problem solve, students think about cause and effect, about actions and consequences, she asserts. Seeley concedes that the PISA results were an appropriate indicator that problem-solving opportunities need to be better integrated into lessons. "We need to give more than lip service to problem solving," she notes, and one way to do that is to create challenging problems that reflect the world that students know.

For example, many students may someday want to convince their parents to take them to an amusement park, such as Disneyland or Disney World. Through an 8-unit lesson for grades 3–5, teams of students learn where to find data to make an informed pitch: they study maps, consider different routes, visit Web sites to get airline schedules and costs, and analyze their data. Each team then presents its vacation plan to the class and discusses the best features of each plan (NCTM, 2005).

Another example: There will be a day when the children who are now in elementary school will have to buy cell phones. Will they "just go with the first plan they come to?" asks Reys. Or will they use their mathematical tools to determine the best plan for them? If students have been taught how to approach a problem and organize data in different ways—to put it into equations or a graph or spreadsheet—they can compare the costs and benefits of each plan and make an informed decision, Reys asserts.

*Will students just go with the first plan they come to? Or will they use mathematical tools to determine which is the best plan?*

That experience will also prepare them for the next issue they'll need to address, she adds. Teachers can ask students to think about the problem-solving process and determine how to use what they learned to make sense of another puzzler. "It's not just about solving this problem," says Reys. "It's also about developing some confidence in their ability to solve other problems."

## Explaining How: Stressing Communication

Another math confidence booster involves communication. When students can explain how they solved a particular problem, when they can discuss their strategies, they solidify their understanding, say educators.

*It's not just about solving this problem. It's also about developing some confidence in their ability to solve other problems.*

"In order to make connections, we have to have conversations about math," states Gail Underwood, a 2nd grade teacher at Grant Elementary School in Columbia, Missouri. Sometimes a discussion is held before an activity, Underwood explains. She asks the students—or they ask each other: Do you have a plan? If you don't have a plan, how can you approach the problem?

The students continue the conversation as they work in pairs or groups (or alone, if preferred) to solve the problem. The group then reconvenes for what Underwood calls a Math Congress. In this forum, students share their strategies and Underwood may introduce math concepts she thinks are important are to discuss. "It's a thoughtful process. There is a purpose," Underwood states.

That purpose includes clarifying thinking and helping students see that there are many approaches to solving a problem, she says. The Math Congress also helps build a sense of community in the classroom. Underwood, who received a 2004 Presidential Award for Excellence in Mathematics and Science Teaching, notes that it takes time, but by October of any given year, her students are usually willing to say to their peers: "This is what I'm thinking," or "I've got two answers, but I'm not sure which one is right, so I'm bringing it to the community."

In doing so, says Underwood, students see themselves as people who make mistakes but who, through discussion, can find a strategy that will lead them to the right response. It's an ongoing life lesson, she observes, because students learn how to ask for help, and, if they see a mistake, they'll know how to correct the result in polite and respectful way.

Emphasizing communication includes giving students more opportunities to write about their mathematical understandings, according to those who crafted the NCTM standards documents. When asked to explain their problem-solving processes or to discuss how the math they learned might be used in the real world, students deepen their understanding of concepts and clarify their thinking (Goldsby & Cozza, 2002; Sjoberg, Slavit, & Coon, 2004).

Students' writing about their thinking also gives teachers alternative methods of assessment and better prepares students for high-stakes tests. In Missouri, for example, a huge portion of the state proficiency test requires that students communicate their thinking, says Underwood. Students have to be able to explain how they came to their conclusions, she states.

## Not Your Mother's Math Class

Underwood's students receive a mathematics education that is vastly different from the one she received. "I don't remember having those discussions about where to start with problem solving," she says. What she does recall is the rote memorization of math facts and worksheets filled with problems that she dutifully completed and turned in, which were corrected (in red ink) and returned—no discussion necessary.

Many of Underwood's colleagues—as well as the parents of her students—had similar experiences. This is one reason that the pace of reform has been sluggish: prudence impedes progress. "How do you help people see that how we did things 20 years ago may not be the right way?" she asks, noting that her experience with school-level instructional change has convinced her that "we have to be thoughtful and careful in how we bring about reform."

One way to reassure those who are anxious is to point out that computation is not ignored when K–6 teachers emphasize algebraic thinking, problem solving, and communication. In the context of solving a problem, for example, a teacher can ask students to recite their times tables and discuss how this knowledge better equips them to solve the problem. It's also appropriate for children to practice computation as a separate activity, so long as "the practice does not become the major activity in mathematics classes," writes Michael T. Battista in "Research and Reform in Mathematics Education" (2001, p. 75). Otherwise, students will come to think that mathematics "involves nothing more than memorizing the rule you must follow to get the right answer," he states (p. 50).

"It's important to acknowledge that computation is an important part of a balanced math program," Seeley agrees. "Even in an era of calculators, we still want kids to do basic arithmetic. They have to have so much more than that, however. They have to know what to do with the arithmetic they learn," she states.

## Relying on Research

Just as students need to know how to apply what they learn, educators need to know how to analyze the results of reforms they implement—and alter the course, if necessary, say experts. Communication between those "who do research in math and those who teach children," must be enhanced, says Saul, who served on the RAND Mathematics Study Panel, which was convened in 1999 to study the lackluster performance in mathematics by U.S. students, determine some of the causes for poor achievement, and identify solutions.

The panel's work culminated in *Mathematical Proficiency for All Students: Toward a Strategic Research and Development Program in Mathematics Education*, a report released to the U.S. Department of Education in 2002. The study suggests that a program of research and development can lead to an increase in students' mathematics proficiency (*see A Cycle of Research, Development, and Improvement, p. 28*). Such a program could help determine

- How to best help teachers acquire the mathematical knowledge they need to effectively teach students from diverse backgrounds.

- The kind of instruction that best helps students become mathematical thinkers and problem solvers.

- How to emphasize algebra from kindergarten through 12th grade.

As pointed out in the report, teaching and learning will improve because such a program institutes a cycle of continuous improvement: there is initial research, development, and improved knowledge and practice, followed by evaluation, which leads to new research, new development, and improved knowledge and practice (RAND Mathematics Study Panel, 2003).

The RAND panel's work coincided with the NCTM's effort to update their original standards. Released in 2000, the new *Principles and Standards* identified priorities that corresponded with the RAND study's conclusions. The new NCTM standards, for example, state that students must develop computational fluency. That ability is included in the description of mathematical proficiency in the RAND report. The NCTM standards also stipulate that by the end of 8th grade, students should have a strong foundation in algebra and geometry. Emphasizing algebra K–12 is a key research focus recommended in the RAND study.

That mathematics researchers and mathematics practitioners should reach similar conclusions about priorities in practice bodes well for improving mathematics education, suggests Seeley, who stresses a need for real collaborations between mathematicians, researchers, and mathematics educators. That way, she notes, "people are working together and learning from each other."

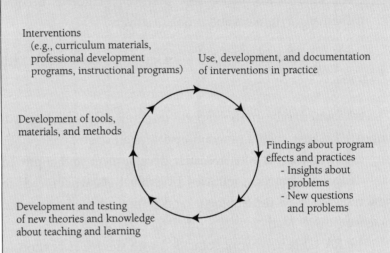

## A Cycle of Research, Development, and Improvement of Practice

Interventions
(e.g., curriculum materials,
professional development
programs, instructional programs)

Use, development, and documentation
of interventions in practice

Development of tools,
materials, and methods

Findings about program
effects and practices
- Insights about
problems
- New questions
and problems

Development and testing
of new theories and knowledge
about teaching and learning

Studies of basic problems of teaching and learning
- Documentation of teaching and learning

*Source:* Adapted from *Mathematical Proficiency for All Students: Toward a Strategic Research and Development Program in Mathematics Education* (p. 6), by the RAND Mathematics Study Panel, 2003, Santa Monica, CA: RAND.

Saul agrees. Such collaboration reinforces what he believes is the essence of standards-based reform: improved student achievement. Conversations between teachers and researchers, Saul says, should be "based on what we want students to learn."

Fortunately, Seeley observes, the underlying theme of the work completed by the RAND panel and NCTM, is that "we all want students to do math better."

# Reflections ◆ ◆ ◆

As many educators point out, the trend toward emphasizing algebraic thinking, problem solving, and communication in K–6 school mathematics is not a new trend. Still, as NCTM's Cathy Seeley acknowledges, "Making that change is pretty challenging." It's helpful, therefore, to keep in mind that

- **Young learners can be high-level learners.** As more teachers implement a standards-based program, they find that their students can more than rise to the challenge. When treated like budding mathematicians, students respond accordingly. As one teacher interviewed for this book observed, "The kids love math because they don't feel threatened by it."

- **Problems can be made relevant to students' lives.** Bring the real world into the classroom. When students wrestle with issues that they will actually encounter throughout their lives, they will see the purpose for learning.

- **Good teaching doesn't come through good luck.** Good teaching results when there is a commitment to continuous improvement. It's important to keep abreast of practices that research shows are effective in helping students learn.

2

# Making Wise Curricular Decisions

*Mathematics allows for no hypocrisy and no vagueness.*

—*Stendhal*

In December 2004, already-beleaguered math educators in the United States no doubt shook their bewildered heads: Was achievement in mathematics among U.S. children improving—or not? On one hand, U.S. 15-year-olds performed poorly in mathematics literacy and problem-solving on the Program for International Student Assessment (PISA). Released in December, PISA results showed that U.S. students ranked well below top-scoring students in Finland and Korea. On the other hand, 4th graders and 8th graders in the United States exceeded international averages in mathematics on the 2003 Trends in International Mathematics and Sciences Study (TIMSS), which was released soon after the PISA.

Any positive performance data is welcome, but it can be misleading. Researchers point out that U.S. 4th graders outperformed their peers in 13 of the other 24 countries participating in the TIMSS study, but U.S. students performed lower than their peers in 11 countries, including Hungary, Japan, the Netherlands, and top-scoring Singapore.

One reason for Singapore's continued strong performance can be traced to that country's curriculum, say researchers. "A mathematically logical, uniform national framework that develops topics in-depth at each grade guides Singapore's mathematics system," reports the American Institutes for Research (Witt, 2005, p. xi).

The importance of developing such a framework—a "more continuous" curriculum—is a lesson that U.S. educators can learn from other countries whose students fare well on international exams, says the NCTM's Cathy Seeley.

Jim Bohan, the K–12 mathematics program coordinator in the Manheim Township School District in Lancaster, Pennsylvania, agrees. An excellent math curriculum should help students deepen their understanding of concepts as they move through the grades, he states. In particular, a mathematics curriculum should be

> Three key principles guide educators as they seek to make curriculum more logical and reasoned—more coherent:
>
> - There must be visible connections between purposes and everyday learning experiences.
> - Learning experiences must be placed in a context that helps the learner understand how those activities, when connected, lead to some larger purpose.
> - The curriculum must take into account and allow for the different ways in which people make sense of their learning experiences. *(See Key Principles for Coherence, p. 38.)*

• **Coherent:** Interrelated mathematical topics should be organized and delivered so that students see the connection among the concepts, procedures, and skills.

• **Focused:** A mathematics curriculum should focus on significant mathematics.

• **Articulated:** A mathematics curriculum should be articulated across the grades so that the students will experience an increased and interrelated understanding of mathematics as they grow through the grades. (Bohan, 2002)

Still, deciding what constitutes "significant" mathematics and determining which concepts to emphasize year to year continues to be a challenge. "As a nation, we don't have a consensus of what should be taught, which makes us very different from other places around the world," observes Barbara Reys, distinguished professor of mathematics education at the University of Missouri. "I'm a believer of a national curriculum, but I don't think I'm in the majority," she says.

Also in the minority is William Schmidt, the U.S. research coordinator for TIMSS and a distinguished professor at Michigan State University. "Why should the content expectations for 4th grade students in Illinois be any different [from] those 4th graders in Alabama or Maryland?" asks Schmidt in *Educational Leadership* (2004, p. 7). Especially now, in this era of No Child Left Behind, it's essential for all educators, in all states, to embrace a set of common standards, Schmidt maintains.

*It's essential for all educators, in all states, to embrace a set of common standards.*

## The Process: Determining What Students Should Learn

For many, the NCTM's *Principles and Standards for School Mathematics* establishes that set of common standards. Indeed, some educators contend that, because many states develop their programs of study around them, the NCTM standards are a de facto U.S. curriculum. (Although the NCTM standards provide guidance, they are not mandated. State frameworks, as a result, differ greatly [Witt, 2005]).

With NCTM, state, or other standards in one hand, educators then often turn to national and state exams to determine the *what*, *when*, and, to some extent, *how* of a mathematics curriculum. In Pennsylvania, for example, a set of assessment anchors, subsets of the NCTM-based Pennsylvania state standards, help

# Perspectives

*Paul Cobb, mathematics education professor at Vanderbilt University, discusses mathematics achievement in the United States with ASCD's Laura Varlas.*

**Q.** In general, math achievement has not improved in the United States. Is there any sign that reforms are having an effect? Are studies like the math results in the 2003 National Assessment of Educational Progress good indicators of an upswing?

**A.** This is really hard to sort out in the absence of studies that focus on what is actually happening in math classrooms. A number of groups will make claims for particular policies they have promoted, but we do not have data on the extent and degree to which they actually have affected teachers' classroom practices, in most cases.

I speculate many teachers learn not to see students' mathematical reasoning because they view their job as covering material. You look for results, the answers. You learn not to be able to focus on how students are reasoning. That's a part of this decoupling of learning from teaching. The recent TIMSS (Trends in International Mathematics and Science Study) Video Study revealed that most U.S. teachers do not attempt to adapt instruction as informed by ongoing assessments of their students' reasoning. Instead, the study found that teachers prepare a lesson plan, have an expectation about how it's going to unfold, and students have to accommodate that. In Japan, it's the other way around. Teachers there continually anticipate what the students are going to do and decide how they can build on that. In that type of lesson plan, thoughts about kids' reasoning are at the center of planning instruction.

Part of our work with teachers is to push them to look at what is happening in mathematics classrooms by focusing on what students actually have to know and do to be viewed as competent. It's just a completely different orientation for math education and education in general.

**Q.** Why does the United States struggle with reproducing some of the successful math strategies popular abroad?

**A.** Look at James Stigler and James Hiebert's book *The Teaching Gap*, which talks about practices of teaching in Japan, as compared to the United States. In Japan, teaching is a knowledge-generating activity so that teaching gradually improves. In this country, we sort of lurch from one reform to the next, where the next one sweeps away everything from the last one, so we're not building. We tend to proceduralize everything, and then we lose the meaning and the intent of it. Take [the Japanese practice of] lesson study for example—[in the United States,] lesson study has been reduced to a formula. But lesson study is a process, a way of continually improving, rather than just a reform to apply. When you listen to arguments for particular instructional approaches or strategies, they're often completely decoupled from how the proposed strategy is going to support learning. We don't relate teaching to learning very well in this country. We tend to rely on ideology, rather than actual hard-earned experiences in classrooms.

*Paul Cobb is the associate director of the National Center for Improving Student Learning and Achievement in Mathematics and Science (NCISLA).*

*Source:* Adapted from "Viewpoint," by L. Varlas, 2004, *Curriculum • Technology Quarterly 13*(3), pp. B–C.

## Key Principles for Coherence

Achieving a coherent, focused, and well-articulated curriculum "involves a number of issues: design, content, connections, and meaning," writes J. A. Beane in *Toward a Coherent Curriculum: The 1995 ASCD Yearbook* (1995, p. 6). According to Beane, three key principles guide educators as they seek to make curriculum more logical and reasoned—more coherent.

• **There must be visible connections between purposes and everyday learning experiences.**

"When adults plan the curriculum, they have to decide not only what its purposes will be, but what kinds of learning experiences will lead toward those purposes," writes Beane (p. 7).

Beane warns that although the planned learning experiences may seem coherent to adults, young people may not sense the same coherence. Educators, therefore, must "persistently maintain the connection between the larger purpose and the specific activity" (p. 7).

"We may say that we want our students to have a sense of the world in which they live, so we introduce statistics to help them understand certain patterns in that world," writes Beane. However, there is always a risk of "disconnecting that work from the real world or, in other words, making it simply an abstract exercise in mathematics" (p. 7).

Abstract versus authentic. Helping students truly grasp what they learn means giving them opportunities to apply what they learn in very real, personal ways.

• **Learning experiences must be placed in a context that helps the learner understand how those activities, when connected, lead to some larger purpose.**

Interdisciplinary studies, curriculum integration, curriculum organized around concepts—these approaches help students see how all the pieces of what they learn fit together.

It's a natural way to organize the curriculum, suggests Beane. When we are confronted with a puzzling situation in real life, he writes, "we hardly stop to think, 'Which part is mathematics, which physical education, which science, which thinking, which valuing, and so on'" (p. 7).

What's more, if we need to find information or acquire new skills to solve a problem, we don't worry about distinctions between disciplines as we do our research. "Understood this way," writes Beane, "knowledge and skills are organically integrated in real life, while their separation in school programs is an artificial and distracting arrangement" (p. 7).

**• The curriculum must take into account and allow for the different ways in which people make sense of their learning experiences.**

Researchers agree that we all seek knowledge and come to understand the world in unique ways. Educators have long been interested in understanding how different theories of learning—from learning styles to multiple intelligences, from constructivism to brain-based learning—should influence curriculum.

Educators must also consider the ways in which a student's culture—ethnicity, class, gender, geography, age, family patterns, and so on—influences how he or she responds to that curriculum. Educators should understand, then, that every learning experience will invoke a wide variety of meanings among students. Thus, the curriculum "must make space for young people to find points of personal engagement," writes Beane. The curriculum must also allow for "the

> ways in which diverse people connect, organize, and make sense out of their experiences" (1995, p. 10).
>
> ---
>
> *Source:* Adapted from *Crafting Curriculum* [online course], by K. Checkley, 2002, Alexandria, VA: Association for Supervision and Curriculum Development.

Bohan determine the "eligible content" for primary and elementary students in his district.

Manheim Township's approach to curriculum development—aligning the district's learning goals with performance outcomes on state assessments—makes sense to many educators. Education consultants Grant Wiggins and Jay McTighe, for example, advocate a three-stage approach to curriculum development that they call "backward" design. "We ask [curriculum] designers to start with a much more careful statement of the desired results—the priority *learnings*—and to derive the curriculum from the performances called for or implied in the goals," write Wiggins and McTighe in *Understanding by Design, Expanded 2nd Edition* (2005, p. 17).

The authors then ask curriculum designers to consider the following questions after framing the goals: What would count as evidence of such achievement? What does it look like to meet these goals? What, then, are the implied *performances* that should make up the assessment, toward which all teaching and learning should point? Only after answering these questions, assert Wiggins and McTighe, "can we logically derive the appropriate teaching and learning experiences so that students might perform successfully to meet the standard" (2005, p. 17).

Such an alignment process is not new. As Wiggins and McTighe point out, respected educator Ralph W. Tyler wrote about planning with the end in mind in *Basic Principles of Curriculum and*

*Instruction*, which was published well before the current standards-based reform movement:

> *Educational objectives become the criteria by which materials*
> *are selected, content is outlined, instructional procedures are*
> *developed, and tests and examinations are prepared. . . .*
> *The purpose of a statement of objectives is to indicate the*
> *kinds of changes in the student to be brought about so that*
> *instructional activities can be planned and developed in a*
> *way likely to attain these objectives.* (1949, pp. 1, 45)

Once the desired changes in the student are identified, educators can then select the curriculum, textbook, or instructional program that can best help teachers help students reach those goals.

## The Process: Selecting Appropriate Materials

*Curriculum, as a concept, as a discrete idea, is almost without boundaries. Curriculum can connote either formal structural arrangements or the substance of what is being taught.*

> —William Toombs and William Tierney, *"Curriculum Definitions*
> *and Reference Points,"* Journal of Curriculum and Supervision

Many options exist for educators who want to provide a standards-based, "intellectually rigorous education for all students in their classes," write Lynn T. Goldsmith and Ilene Kantrov in *Guiding Curriculum Decisions for Middle-Grades Mathematics* (2001, p. 3). It wasn't always that way. Faced with a dearth of materials when the NCTM standards were first released in 1989, many teachers had to develop their own lessons and activities.

*Helping children see how mathematics fits into their everyday lives is the best thing teachers can do for students.*

Now, with so many programs available, what's most important is an understanding of what makes for a sound school mathematics curriculum, the authors state, adding that "before you can judge a curriculum's potential for promoting academic excellence, you need to know what to base your judgments on" (Goldsmith & Kantrov, 2001, p. 7). Goldsmith and Kantrov evaluate curriculum materials by looking at three components:

• **Academic rigor.** This is defined by the standards, Goldsmith and Kantrov contend. "An academically rigorous curriculum articulates a clear set of goals for learning" (2001, p. 9).

• **Equity.** Curriculum materials that are equitable promote "high levels of achievement among a wide range of students," state Goldsmith and Kantrov. To do so, curricula should include "approaches and activities that accommodate a variety of learning styles" and give students many ways to access information and "grapple with important ideas of the subject area," write the authors (2001, pp. 12, 13).

• **Developmental Appropriateness.** To be developmentally appropriate, curriculum materials must honor how children learn best at each grade level. Additionally, write Goldsmith and Kantrov, the curricula must appeal to students' interests. "Students are more likely to put effort into their schoolwork" when the lessons and activities are "interesting, important, and relevant to their lives" (2001, p. 15).

# What to Ask When You're Looking

The NCTM doesn't endorse any mathematics curricula. Still, the association asks that educators pose the following questions when determining if a curriculum, textbook, or instructional plan reflects the goals of an NCTM standards-based learning program:

• Do the teaching materials ask students to perform at high cognitive levels? In other words, states NCTM's Cathy Seeley, educators need to know if the materials are challenging students and helping them stretch to new levels of understanding. Does the curriculum call for higher-level skills?

Students must learn to "think more deeply and solve more complex problems," Seeley states. They must develop an analytical ability. Students will be taking jobs in the future that "don't even exist now," she adds. "A person needs to be adaptable and ready to transfer their skills." Students, therefore, need a curriculum that will help them develop deep general skills, including the ability to think and take problems apart.

• Do the materials help teachers understand the content for themselves and foster a better understanding of the teaching and learning of mathematics? Teachers may have a strong math background, but they need to know how students best learn mathematics, too. A good curriculum can give teachers that guidance, Seeley states.

"The materials should help us grow our own understanding so we can ask the questions that will help students grow," she says. With a good curriculum, Seeley contends, some aspects of mathematical concepts can be deepened and can help teachers see new ways to present the information to help students.

• Do the materials integrate assessment into the teaching and learning process? Assessment cannot be viewed as the big test, Seeley states. An effective curriculum will provide ideas for ongoing assessment, she contends.

Teachers should be continually gauging what students know, says Seeley, "so we can catch problems early and better guide student learning."

## Standards-Based Math: Interesting, Important, and Relevant

Helping children see how mathematics fits into their every day lives is one of the best things teachers can do for their students, states LeeAnn Cervini, a K–5 enrichment specialist at Terry A. Taylor Elementary School in Spencerport, New York. Cervini was a 1st grade teacher when her district went in search for a standards-based curriculum. The district selected *Investigations in Number, Data, and Space* because "it featured a constructivist approach to teaching math," Cervini says.

*Investigations* is one of three elementary curricula that are based on the NCTM's standards, according to the K–12 Mathematics Curriculum Center (K–12 MCC). The other elementary programs are *Everyday Math* and *Math Trailblazers* (*see Summing Them Up, p. 46*).

### Investigations in Number, Data, and Space

Teachers at Travell Elementary School in Ridgewood, New Jersey, use *Investigations* because the curriculum poses problems that require children "to think deeply about the mathematics involved," states Ashley Berk, a 5th grade teacher at Travell. "This program, when implemented well, really helps students under-stand mathematics." The lessons and activities are based on students' thinking processes, she explains, adding that the children "are not just performing mathematical tasks and algorithms; they are using reasoning to arrive at a response. And, the process by which they arrived at that response is highly valued."

For example, in a 5th grade level exercise called How Many Cubes?, students are asked to predict how many boxes of ornaments will fit into a larger shipping box. Students know that one ornament per box equals one cube, and they work together to arrive at a general method for determining how many of those cubes will fit into boxes of various sizes (TERC, n.d.). An important aspect of this kind of lesson is for students to discuss their strategies as the problem becomes increasingly complex. "We ask students to describe and show the different methods they use," Berk explains. "In doing so, they clarify their own thinking and also, perhaps, that of their classmates."

## Everyday Math

Linda Figgins, a 6th grade teacher, began her career at McKin-ley Elementary School in Elgin, Illinois, more than 30 years ago. In that time, she has seen how important it is for schools to secure teacher support for any kind of reform. As a result, when her school went in search of a standards-based math program, Figgins used grant money from the National Science Foundation to fund a teacher-led exploration of the curricula available to them. "We surveyed all of the best curricula out there and ended up select-ing *Everyday Math*," she says. The reason: She and her colleagues felt the program offered teacher-friendly materials and support—key ingredients to implementing an instructional approach that requires drastic change.

## Summing Them Up
### *Why These Programs Work*

There are many good standards-based mathematics programs to choose from. At the K–12 Mathematic Curriculum Center (K–12 MCC), there are descriptions of 12 comprehensive mathematics education programs, developed with National Science Foundation funding, that align well with the National Council of Teachers of Mathematics' Curriculum and Evaluation Standards for School Mathematics (1989) and the Principles and Standards for School Mathematics (2000).

Established in 1997 by the Education Development Center, the K–12 MCC Web site (www.edc.org/mcc) contains up-to-date information on those curricula, including three elementary-level programs:

• *Investigations in Number, Data, and Space* is a K–5 mathematics program that focuses on computational fluency with whole number operations, the structure of the base-10 number system, the meaning of fractions, representing and describing data, examining two- and three-dimensional shapes, measuring, and change over time. The *Investigations* program was developed at TERC and is based on an extensive body of research on how students learn mathematics.

In each unit, students explore the central topics in depth through a series of investigations, encountering and using important mathematical ideas. Students actively engage in mathematical reasoning to solve complex mathematical problems. They represent, explain, and justify their thinking using mathematical tools and appropriate technology, including calculators, as a natural part of their work.

*Investigations* provides meaningful, repeated practice of basic facts and skills through the use of activities and games. The investigations allow significant time for students to think about the problems and to model, draw, write, and talk with peers and the teacher about their mathematical thinking. Students work as a whole class, individually, in pairs, and in small groups.

• *Everyday Mathematics* is a pre-K–6 curriculum that builds on fundamental mathematical strands such as numeration and order; measures and measurement; reference frames; operations; patterns, functions, and sequences; data and chance; geometry and spatial sense; and algebra and the use of variables.

The curriculum integrates mathematics into other subject areas; mathematics becomes part of ongoing classroom routines, outdoor play, and transitional moments that occur every day. Teachers use *Everyday Mathematics* as a core curriculum during class math time. They also incorporate mathematical ideas and routines throughout the school day and encourage the children to continue the routines at home with their families.

The *Everyday Mathematics* curriculum is based on research that suggests that people rarely learn new concepts or skills the first time they experience them but fully understand them only after repeated exposures. Students in the program study important concepts over consecutive years; each grade level builds on and extends conceptual understandings established in prior grades.

• A fundamental principle of *Math Trailblazers* is that mathematics is best learned through active solving of real problems. Lessons are grounded in everyday situations, so abstractions build on experience. Students' skills, procedures, and concepts emerge and develop as they solve complex problems.

The curriculum introduces challenging content at every grade level, including computation, measurement, data collection, statistics, geometry, ratio, probability, graphing, simple algebra, estimation, mental arithmetic, and patterns and relationships. Each grade level has 16–20 units; units range from one to three weeks long.

A central tenet of *Math Trailblazers* is that real problems are naturally interdisciplinary. The curriculum integrates mathematics with many disciplines, especially science and language arts. Students explore situations by drawing pictures; gathering, organizing, graphing data; and analyzing their results. And, as part of every lesson, students discuss and write about mathematics.

*Source:* Adapted from *Curriculum Summaries* (7th ed.), by the K–12 Mathematics Curriculum Center at Education Development Center, 2004. The work was supported by National Science Foundation. Retrieved May 27, 2005, from www2.edc.org/mcc /curricula.asp

*For mathematics to be meaningful, teachers must provide a context that helps children understand the concepts.*

"Standards-based math, in general, is a very different way of teaching math," Figgins observes, adding that it's not always easy to incorporate a "child-learning perspective" into lessons and activities. For mathematics to be meaningful, for example, teachers must know how to provide a context that helps children understand the concepts. One way *Everyday Math* achieves this is by using children's own lives to show how the mathematics applies to them.

In one 6th grade lesson in which students apply their understanding of mean, median, and mode, for example, students gather data on how many minutes they spend in the shower or bath, how long it takes them to read 10 pages in a book, how many hours of television they watch each week, and so on. They then plot their data along a line, from the least number of minutes spent on an activity to the greatest number of minutes spent. The catch: They don't label their plot lines. Another student must determine which number would most likely correspond with the activities the student charted (University of Chicago Mathematics Project, 2003).

A challenge with *Everyday Math*, however, is that the curriculum is organized in a spiral form, says Figgins. That means a topic students encounter in grade 2 will reappear in the curriculum in the following grades, but at higher levels of complexity. Teachers may be uncomfortable with moving on to a new concept "before [they] think all children have mastered the content," she states; teachers must learn to trust that when students revisit the concept, they'll have plenty of opportunities for review and practice, Figgins says.

## Math Trailblazers

In the 27 years she has spent teaching 2nd grade, Mary Short has seen many changes in the way mathematics is taught in schools. Children today don't just do procedures, for example. They use manipulatives and hands-on experiences to see "how math works," she states.

That's one of the strong elements of the *Math Trailblazers* curriculum, says Short, who uses the program with her students at Long Neck Elementary School in Millsboro, Delaware. Another appealing feature is that *Math Trailblazers* builds lessons around objects students see regularly in their world. Students can learn an "enormous amount of math" using buttons, for example. "Students can sort the buttons by color, shape, size, number of holes, and so on," Short explains. They can create a data table, indicating the number of small, medium, and large buttons they have; students can then graph those amounts. They can use buttons to create math problems. The possibilities are endless, says Short,

Name _____ Date _____

# Miko's Tile Design

Miko made this design using color tiles. She wrote this number sentence to describe it.
1 + 2 + 3 + 2 + 1 = 9

Her friend Amy wrote another number sentence for the design. 1 + 3 + 5 = 9

**1.** Tell how Miko and Amy were looking at the design when they wrote these number sentences.

Miko

_____

_____



Amy

_____

_____

**2.** Write a different number sentence to describe Miko's design.

_____

**Tile Designs**                    **SG · Grade 2 · Unit 2 · Lesson 1** 23

who also appreciates that the lessons allow for many ways to solve problems.

In the 2nd grade lesson Tile Designs, for instance, children make designs with color tiles and then write number sentences to describe them (*see A Cycle of Research, Development, and Improvement, p. 28*). When students share their number sentences, they see different ways to write the problems. In an extension activity, one student will write a number sentence and then challenge another student to create a tile design for that sentence (Tile Designs, 2005).

Children love math when they have these kinds of activities "because they don't feel threatened by them," Short affirms. Students learn that there are different strategies for coming up with an answer—and that's okay. "They explore, take risks, they share, and they gain a lot of confidence in their ability to do math as well." The program, says Short, in short, "is phenomenal."

## Homegrown Standards-Based Approaches

Whether district administrators or individual teachers decide to use one of the curricula described on the K–12 MCC Web site, it's likely that adhering to state or district standards will require that they make some modifications to the learning plan, say experts. "Until we have a national curriculum, there will never be a single program that will solve the curriculum issues for every state," says John Van de Walle, professor emeritus at Virginia Commonwealth University. And, despite a push for the NCTM to propose a national curriculum, "Every state seems perfectly happy to make their own standards, no matter what other states are doing," observes Van de Walle, who is also a consultant and mathematics education author

## When the Textbook Is the Curriculum

Barbara J. Reys agrees that you'll never find one textbook to meet all the needs teachers have. Still, the textbook "ought to provide a good base so teachers don't always have to search for things to enrich their curriculum," she maintains.

When Reys taught 20 years ago, textbooks were a lot alike. She spent a lot of time, therefore, helping teachers create standards-based materials to enrich their lessons. "And we'd always say, 'What if someone would just write a good textbook?'"

Someone has, according to Reys. She points out that there is a lot of variety now. "If you want to keep a traditional approach, there are books like that. If you want to do something different, there are textbooks for that and you can push to adopt these kinds of materials," she says.

Reys is even hopeful that the standards-based textbooks will be used as a catalyst for reform in some districts. "The textbook has a big impact on what kids get to study and how teachers teach—it can change dynamics of classroom," Reys states. Textbooks, she insists, can be change agents.

(*Elementary and Middle School Mathematics: Teaching Developmentally*, 5th edition [2003, Allyn & Bacon]).

As a result, many teachers will select activities from a variety of sources to help students attain the learning objectives spelled out in their state or district standards. In Gwinnett County, Georgia, for example, Leanne Luttrell creates her own lessons, relying on the textbook as a resource only. Luttrell, who teaches 4th and 5th grade gifted students as well as students in two advanced math classes at Sycamore Elementary School in Sugar Hill, uses lessons from *Investigations* and adapts lesson ideas she finds when attending state

# Finding a Better Book

The U.S. textbook is getting better. Several elementary, middle, and high school mathematics textbooks are now aligned with NCTM standards and current research on learning. Approximately 10–15 percent of U.S. classrooms currently use these standards-based textbooks.

These textbooks differ from traditional mathematics textbooks in that they present mathematical ideas in various contexts and engage students in exploring ideas, solving problems, sharing strategies, and building new knowledge based on solid conceptual understanding. Teachers no longer simply cover material. Rather, they facilitate a classroom learning environment that encourages questioning, conjecturing, and problem formulation and values student thinking and multiple strategies.

Given the prominent role of mathematics textbooks, making a wise selection is crucial because it determines the scope of mathematics that students experience and, to some extent, how teachers present the material and how students learn. Teachers and administrators involved with selecting mathematics textbooks should be familiar with the characteristics associated with standards-based mathematics curricula and textbooks should present material coherently, develop ideas in depth, promote sense making, engage students, and motivate learning.

To effectively assess a textbook, educators should address the following questions:

• What key mathematical ideas in each content strand should each grade level address?

• How does the content of the textbook align with these key mathematical ideas?

• What types of activities does the textbook provide? Are students challenged to think and develop understanding, or are they simply shown how to work some exercises and then asked to practice procedures? Will these activities engage students in mathematical thinking and activity?

• Is there a focus on mathematical thinking and problem solving? Are students expected to explain "why"? Does the textbook encourage students to explore "what if" questions and offer and test conjectures?

*Source:* From "Mathematics Textbooks Matter," by B. J. Reys, R. E. Reys, and O. Chávez, 2004, *Educational Leadership 61*(5), pp. 64–65.

and national mathematics conferences. Such inventiveness, says Luttrell, requires that she really know her math. To pull together activities from a large variety of resources requires that she sees the connections among the concepts covered in those activities, she suggests.

Jennifer Buttars, a 2nd grade teacher, is equally as versatile. At Columbia Elementary School in West Jordan, Utah, Buttars must ensure that her students, among other things, learn how to add and subtract double digit numbers, begin studying fractions, solidify their number sense, continue building their mathematics vocabulary, begin geometry, do some measurement and coordinate graphing, and continue building their algebraic understanding. These outcomes are part of Utah's state core for 2nd grade and are based on the five content standards from NCTM, Buttars explains. To address these various content areas, Buttars uses *Investigations*, along with NCTM activities—primarily from the *Navigations* series. Her students also work on a daily word

# The Tech Connection
## *Software That Supports Thinking*

### *By Mary Santilli*

Want to get elementary students excited about mathematics and have them acquire technological savvy at the same time? Here are some excellent resources for the classroom computer or for the entire computer lab in your school. *Math Arena*, *Ten Tricky Tiles*, and *The Logical Journey of the Zoombinis* are three software selections that will enrich any math class.

## Keep Them Coming Back for More

For grades 2–5, *Math Arena* by Sunburst is a terrific tool for most concepts covered in the upper elementary grades. *Math Arena* offers a collection of 10 Time Trials and 10 BuZZin activities that will keep students interested and coming back to learn more. Children have the opportunity to compete against a clock or another player. They even have the choice to turn off the timer to explore problems and develop strategies at their own pace. Once students develop confidence and skills, they can modify the level of play to attempt more challenging problems. Players accumulate points as they go through the program, allowing a teacher to easily follow a child's progress.

Favorite *Math Arena* Time Trials include the following:

• Array Reversal requires students to create multiplication arrays within a 100 frame. They must try to cover the grid without any spaces or gaps.

• Flipster asks students to use geometric flips, slides, and rotations to match a given tile with the same pattern that is positioned differently within a 3 x 3 grid of randomly arranged characters.

• Percent Crossing challenges students by altering the percent of height increases or decreases necessary for a bug to cross between moving platforms. This is perfect for students exploring decimals and percents.

• The Splat Degree challenge uses a flyswatter rotating at 15-degree intervals. The goal is to swat the fly in the fewest moves possible. Students develop meaningful strategies for understanding spatial sense in relation to degree of angle and have a lot of fun in the process.

Whereas *Math Arena's* Time Trial activities are centered on problem solving, the BuZZin activities focus on predicting, estimating, identifying number relationships, and computation in activities such as Fraction/Match, Equalizer, and Budget Breaker. Other BuZZin activities include

• The Predictor. This activity focuses on probability, but with a novel twist. Children buzz in when they think they have enough information to predict how many of the 100 flowers will be blue as the garden blooms one flower at a time. This is a great activity for teaching percentages.

• The Price Slasher. In this game, everything is on sale. This activity is great for calculating varying percentages off given amounts.

Finally, *Math Arena* throws a curve ball at the experienced user with the Tri-Mathlon. Here, students experience a series of three 30-second Time Trials or BuZZins played in succession. A teacher management tool is available to create reports on individual students or teams for any or all of the activities.

## A Home Run for Computation

*Ten Tricky Tiles*, originally developed by Marcy Cook, helps children understand number puzzles and offers gentle assistance when necessary. The activities on this disk include Addition & Subtraction, Balance Tiles, and Crossword Tiles.

In the Addition & Subtraction game, students are given five number sentences, both vertically and horizontally oriented, with many missing addends and subtrahends. Operations are identified for students to determine values. Students decide where to place the 10 tiles (0–9) in the equations. Some equations are easy to solve because there is only one missing addend. Other equations are more challenging. If a child needs assistance, there are 10 hints available to help solve the number sentences. This is a great strategy game and one that is very easy for children to master. There is also a built-in calculator to check facts on any of the levels.

The next level of Ten Tricky Tiles is Balance Tiles. In this activity, children use a more algebraic approach to solving addition and subtraction problems. The screen shows three horizontally oriented number sentences with missing addends, and students quickly realize they must make both sides of the equation balance. This is a good introduction to algebraic thinking.

Finally, the most challenging activity in Ten Tricky Tiles is Crossword Tiles. In this interconnected puzzle of vertical and horizontal tiles, children have to carefully place the 0–9 tiles in the correct spaces to solve the problem. Students have to use a very logical approach to correctly solve any of these problems. If any one number is incorrectly placed, it affects the solutions to all of the problems in the crossword.

## Challenges at Different Levels

The final software recommendation is *The Logical Journey of the Zoombinis* from Riverdeep. Designed for grades 2–5, this program caters to a variety of ability levels designated as "Not So Easy," "Very Hard," "Oh So Hard," and, finally, "Very, Very Hard." At each level opportunities for solid student engagement and rich classroom discussion abound as children trek with the imaginary Zoombinis—characters with wild glasses, weird hairdos, and springy shoes—in distant lands and learn such concepts as graphing, data analysis, classifying, patterns, and functions. I recommend the patterns, graphing, and attribute-sorting activities for younger students and the grouping, logical thinking, and algebraic thinking for older students.

*Math Arena, Ten Tricky Tiles,* and *The Logical Journey of the Zoombinis* are just some of the resources available to make mathematics meaningful and appropriately challenging for children in elementary school. Add some zest to your mathematics class by introducing one or more of these terrific tools.

*Mary Santilli (SantillM@trumbullps.org) is the math program leader for Trumbull Public Schools in Connecticut.*

*Source:* From "Elementary Math Software That Makes Kids Think," by M. Santilli, 2004, *Curriculum•Technology Quarterly 13*(3), pp. 7–8.

problem, taken from the Jordan School District daily review resource (which she co-wrote). One such problem is called The Number of the Day, she says. The concept is simple: Every day, Buttars' students have to create number sentences whose sums are equivalent to that day's number. If the number of the day is *120*, for example, students would write *60 plus 60* or *119 plus 1*, and so on. Students then use a calculator to check their work.

Buttars will soon be moving to 6th grade. Her ability to create a program by first examining expected student outcomes will help make the transition easier. "The first thing I did was access our state office Web sites and took the 6th grade math test," Buttars says. "As I went through the test, I would ask, 'How could I teach this? Do I know it well enough to go deep with it?'"

These kinds of questions that teachers ask themselves are, in the end, what make any curriculum effective, say educators. "When you see successful teachers, you see teachers who have rethought the way to handle the curriculum," says Seeley.

## Reflections ◆ ◆ ◆

In ancient times, farmers harvested their grain by holding their stalks of wheat into the wind. The chaff would blow away, leaving the kernels intact.

When selecting the right curriculum for your school or district, you're very much like ancient farmers. To help you separate the wheat from the chaff,

• **Know your standards.** Selecting an appropriate curriculum for a district or school is not an individual endeavor, nor are decisions made in isolation from national imperatives and concerns. It's helpful for all members of the math curricula committee to read as many relevant standards documents as possible—NCTM's, the state's, the district's—and consider how these sources are interrelated.

• **Know your educational philosophy and instructional approach.** Ask questions such as, What kinds of learning experiences do we want our students to have? Which of the curricular options provide for these experiences?

• **Understand the curriculum development process.** If it's been awhile since you learned about scope and sequence, alignment, articulation, continuity, and so on, a quick refresher course may be in order.

3

# Bringing the Curriculum to Life in the Classroom

*If I am given a formula, and I am*
*ignorant of its meaning, it cannot*
*teach me anything . . .*

—*St. Augustine,* De Magistro

*Passive learning is an oxymoron.*
*—John Van de Walle*

Breaking with tradition is absolutely essential if teachers are to effectively teach standards-based mathematics, say many educators. Tradition-bound teachers have long used a didactic approach: "The teacher shows the students something—maybe with a manipulative—and then students try it," says John Van de Walle, professor emeritus at Virginia Commonwealth University. If this pattern of the teacher demonstrating, the students practicing procedures continues, he warns, students soon will focus only on the rules they must follow, not on understanding why those rules work.

Conversely, says Van de Walle, "a forward-looking teacher is one who will say to students, 'OK, we're going to do this problem today and it involves adding fractions.'" The teacher doesn't immediately give the students an algorithm to follow (find the common denominator and then add), he explains. Instead, the teacher may use an entire class period to focus on one or two problems. The teacher may ask students to create pictures of the quantities suggested by the fractions and discuss what quantity they think will result when they bring the parts of two wholes together. This approach helps students discover how math makes sense, Van de Walle asserts. It's a method that "is closer to that which is used in higher-achieving countries around the world," he says, adding that it's still not clear how long it will be before such practice is the norm in the United States.

Such practices are the norm for the teachers interviewed for this book. These teachers have broken with tradition and they have the 2004 Presidential Award for Excellence in Mathematics and Science Teaching to show for it. In this chapter, these innovative teachers describe how they help students make sense of mathematics and bring the standards-based curriculum to life in their classrooms.

## A Standards-Based Approach to Teaching Mathematics

*Mathematical rigor is like clothing; in its style it ought to suit the occasion, and it diminishes comfort and restrains freedom of movement if it is either too loose or too tight.*

—*G. F. Simmons*

NCTM's *Principles and Standards for School Mathematics* spells out broad learning goals for K–12 students in 10 different categories. The first five standards present goals in the mathematical content areas; the second five describe goals for problem solving, reasoning and proof, connections, communication, and representation (NCTM, 2005). As the lesson ideas presented here illustrate, teachers have many ways to help students attain these learning objectives. What also becomes obvious is that it's difficult for these standards to be addressed in isolation; each of the lesson ideas, as a result, addresses more than one standard.

## Numbers and Operations

▶ Understand numbers, ways of representing numbers, relationships among numbers, and number systems.

▶ Understand meanings of operations and how they relate to one another.

▶ Compute fluently and make reasonable estimates.

Standards are listed with the permission of the National Council of Teachers of Mathematics (NCTM). NCTM does not endorse the content or validity of these alignments.

In *The Brain and Mathematics: Making Number Sense*, an ASCD video-based professional development program, cognitive neuropsychologist Brian Butterworth defines number sense as having a "sense of the manyness"—the numerosity—of a collection of things. According to Butterworth, children come to school with a "numerical startup kit," and activities in school build on that foundation (D'Arcangelo, 2001). In other words, our natural sense of numbers develops with our experiences throughout childhood and is the basis for the mathematical learning.

*Our natural sense of numbers develops with our experiences throughout childhood.*

Francine Plotycia, a 2nd grade teacher at Abingdon Elementary School in Abingdon, Maryland, understands the importance of honing students' number sense, so a regular feature of her math lessons gives students a chance to do some mental math to help them see numbers in different ways. She holds up large index cards with dot stickers that show different configurations of a number, for example, then asks, "What does a group of 10 dots look like as compared to a group of 7 dots?" Plotycia then uses the dots to show simple addition or subtraction sentences. Students see that the number 3 results when she removes 7 dots from a group of 10 dots; students observe that the same result occurs when Plotycia removes 4 dots from a group of 7 dots. This activity can extend into a game using dominoes or dice; students write addition or subtraction sentences based on the numbers that appear after tossing the dominoes.

Plotycia also likes to have students compose and decompose numbers. "It helps them see that 50 is not just 5 tens, but also 3 tens and 20 ones, or 10 fives," she says. And that leads into building on their knowledge of regrouping. In 1st grade, her students had been exposed to regrouping with addition. Now they tackle subtracting two-digit numbers. "We use unifix cubes—little squares that fit together—and students physically do the regrouping so they can make sense of it, so they can see what it is—there's nothing abstract about it." As students work with their squares (they each have a bag of 1,000 cubes), Plotycia circulates the room, asking questions such as, "Did the number of cubes in the 'ones' group change?" "Did the tens place value change?" "Did the original number change?"

Through activities like this, students' tactile understanding will eventually move into the abstract and they'll be able to readily add or subtract numbers using an algorithm rather than a manipulative, Plotycia states.

Gail Underwood's 2nd grade students in Columbia, Missouri, take on a business problem to help them better understand the base-10 number system. The students at Grant Elementary School must help Underwood's "Aunt Mary" determine how to best package the homemade candy she sells to organizations. Should she process the orders in packages of 2, 3, 4, or 10? What makes the most sense?

Students work in groups to determine the best packaging option for the money. They then write letters to Aunt Mary, explaining why they think their packaging plan makes sense. Aunt Mary will eventually call the students and let them know that, because it will save her money on packaging and shipping, she plans to mail her candy in packages of 10.

"That becomes the model," Underwood explains: A new package is created when Aunt Mary has made and wrapped 10 pieces of candy. Underwood's students will draw the package—it becomes a rectangle—and they know the package represents 10 single pieces.

Getting to know numbers and place value is critical if students are to grasp more complex mathematical relationships, say educators. "Learning mathematics is a cumulative process," states Butterworth in the video *The Brain and Mathematics: Making Number Sense* (2001). If students "fail to understand one stage, then anything that's built upon that stage is going to be rather fragile," he points out.

If an understanding is shaky, however, many educators advise that students be given opportunities to represent concepts visually. When teaching students how to differentiate between tenths and hundredths, for instance, 5th grade teacher Ashley Berk asks her students to use a 10 x 10 grid to make a visual representation of a decimal. "If the decimal were 0.2, kids would shade in two columns on the grid," says Berk, who teaches at Travell Elementary School in Ridgewood, New Jersey.

"The lesson appeals to various types of learners," she explains. There's a visual piece, a kinesthetic piece, and an interpersonal piece—students work on the game with others. The activity also requires students to do some reflective writing—when they finish, students determine and write about what they did well and what they needed to work on.

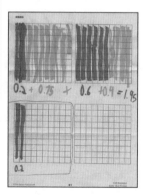

*Students use a 10 x 10 grid to make a visual representation of a decimal.*

## Algebra

▶ Understand patterns, relations, and functions.

▶ Represent and analyze mathematical situations and structures using algebraic symbols.

▶ Use mathematical models to represent and understand quantitative relationships.

▶ Analyze change in various contexts.

Standards are listed with the permission of the National Council of Teachers of Mathematics (NCTM). NCTM does not endorse the content or validity of these alignments.

*All the patterning, classification, addition, and subtraction build an understanding of relationships and reciprocity— a foundation that supports algebraic thinking.*

The NCTM believes that all students should have a solid foundation in algebraic thinking before they head to high school. Building algebraic understanding is something that begins, "as soon as you enter school," states the NCTM's president, Cathy Seeley. Which is important because, in addition to better preparing them for formal high school algebra courses, helping younger students develop algebraic thinking hones "a tremendous life skill that many of our young people haven't been developing for a number of years," Seeley maintains. "Algebraic thinking goes beyond solving equations and figuring out the slope of a line," she explains. Algebraic understanding allows people to "process information by categorizing things that have similar mathematical qualities and making generalizations of them. That's a skill that's used throughout schooling." Indeed, it's a skill that helps students develop an understanding of cause and effect, of actions and consequences, Seeley says. This way of thinking overflows into other areas, such as science and even global decision making, she states. She goes on to say that algebraic thinking is about relationships and logical thinking. So, when students hear about the federal deficit, for example, understanding cause and effect will help them make a more-informed decision about whether to support a tax cut, Seeley suggests.

Teachers in the primary grades need to understand "all of the work we do that supports algebraic thinking," Underwood explains. All the patterning, classification, addition and subtraction—these all build an understanding of relationships and reciprocity, she says.

Students do a lot with patterning in kindergarten and 1st grade. Underwood helps her 2nd graders build on that knowledge base by introducing patterns that grow. "I like to use coloring on the hundreds board to demonstrate repeating patterns and growing patterns. Patterns get at functions," she says.

Basic computation can also begin a student's journey in algebraic thinking. "We split numbers apart and put them together in different ways," explains Jennifer Buttars, a 2nd grade teacher at Columbia Elementary School in West Jordan, Utah. "We look at the equal sign and make sure that what's on one side is equal to what is on the other side." She does this by posing simple addition or subtraction sentences. "It can be as simple as asking students, Two plus what is the same as five? Then, if you write out $2 + \square = 5$, that's not too far from $2 + X = 5$," she says. "Algebra formalizes algebraic thinking."

Students often don't believe that they have the knowledge to do formal algebra, adds Berk. She recently wrote an equation on the board—such as $X + 3 = 2 \times X$—and her 5th grade students' mouths just dropped open, according to Berk. Then she erased the X and placed a box in the sentence: $\square + 3 = 2 \times \square$. Her students were relieved and realized they could plug in numbers solve the puzzle. Berk explained to her students that the box, which they were accustomed to seeing, could be replaced with an X and that the process for arriving at an answer remained the same. "A few days later, I used the X instead of the box, and they were able to work with the variable," she says. "I just gave them time to become comfortable with the notation."

Leanne Luttrell, who teaches 4th and 5th grade gifted students at Sycamore Elementary School in Sugar Hill, Georgia, also introduces formal algebra gradually. She uses a scale to emphasize the point that the equal sign symbolizes balance. The manipulative helps Luttrell's students see, very concretely, that if they add or subtract something from one side, they also have to add or subtract it from the other side to remain balanced. Students enjoy doing concrete activities, Luttrell maintains. They "grow to love manipulatives because when you're teaching that way, they understand it," she says.

---

### Geometry

▶ Analyze characteristics and properties of two- and three-dimensional geometric shapes and develop mathematical arguments about geometric relationships.

▶ Specify locations and describe spatial relationships using coordinate geometry and other representational systems.

▶ Apply transformations and use symmetry to analyze mathematical situations.

▶ Use visualization, spatial reasoning, and geometric modeling to solve problems.

Standards are listed with the permission of the National Council of Teachers of Mathematics (NCTM). NCTM does not endorse the content or validity of these alignments.

---

An activity designed to help students consider patterns proved to be a natural way for 1st grade teacher Cynthia Cliche to integrate algebraic thinking and geometric understanding. Her students at Homer Pittard Campus School in Murfreesboro, Tennessee, make a new paper quilt every month. One month, Cliche's students created panels for a flower quilt theme; another month the theme was raindrops. When each month's tapestry is assembled, Cliche asks her students to look for patterns and shapes. What shapes are included in the flowers' designs? Do the borders have a repeating pattern? What shapes are used in the borders—squares, rectangles, diamonds?

Cliche and her students then worked together to find the area and perimeter of their tapestry as they put their panels together. When they display the quilt on the wall in the hallway, the children document and display what they have deduced about area and perimeter and what they have noticed about the patterns was documented and posted next to that month's quilt. "I want people understand that the quilt isn't just a 'pretty' design," Cliche explains. "I want them to see that they're mathematical—there is math going on in those quilts!"

Cliche's activity, which requires students to recognize shapes as well as patterns, is essential to helping students develop geometric reasoning; it is a first step in the developmental march toward a deep understanding of geometry. (The activity assumes that students are at level 0 of Van Hiele's levels of geometric thought [*see Van Hiele's Levels of Geometric Reasoning, p. 74*]).

*This isn't just a pretty design, says Cliche. When her 1st grade students create tapestries, they learned about area, perimeter, patterns, and shapes.*

Beth Peters, a 3rd grade teacher at Village East Elementary in Aurora, Colorado, uses an activity called The Caterpillar's Birthday to integrate algebra and geometry and also help students hone their problem-solving skills. She tells students that a caterpillar on his first birthday has a square body, a triangle-shaped head, and a triangle-shaped tail, with a triangle-shaped spine on each side of his boxy body. Each year, Peters says, the caterpillar will grow by one square and two spines—the head and tail remain constant. How many squares will be on the caterpillar's body when he turns 10? How many triangles will be on his body?

Children determine how they would approach the problem— one child might draw a caterpillar with 10 boxes and 20 spines, for example; another child might decide to create a T-chart, plugging in data for each year. "This activity is very successful for

*Some of Beth Peters' students drew a diagram.*

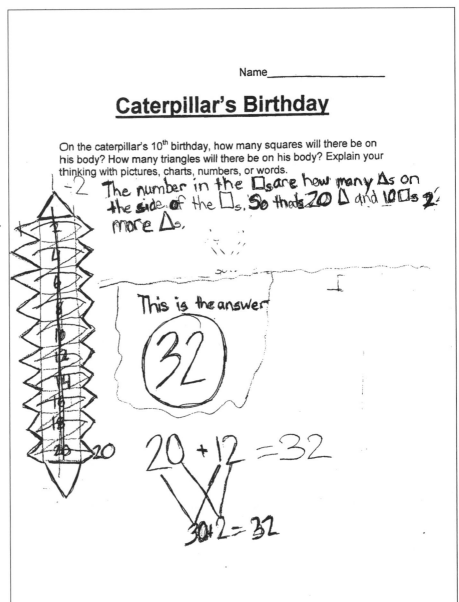

Name_____

## Caterpillar's Birthday

On the caterpillar's 10th birthday, how many squares will there be on his body? How many triangles will there be on his body? Explain your thinking with pictures, charts, numbers, or words.

The number in the □s are how many △s on the side of the □s. So thats 20 △ and 10 □s 2 more △s.

This is the answer
32

20 + 12 = 32

30 + 2 = 32

every mathematician in the classroom," Peters says. Each of the approaches students use yield valid responses and reveal how they came to understand the problem and the concepts it addresses.

Name_____

# Caterpillar's Birthday

On the caterpillar's 10th birthday, how many squares will there be on his body? How many triangles will there be on his body? Explain your thinking with pictures, charts, numbers, or words.

It is the number 22 triangle because I use the tichar

*Others used a T-chart to organize data.*

| Birthday | Triagles | squares |
|---|---|---|
| 1 | 4 | 1 |
| 2 | 6 | 2 |
| 3 | 8 | 3 |
| 4 | 10 | 4 |
| 5 | 12 | 5 |
| 6 | 14 | 6 |
| 7 | 16 | 7 |
| 8 | 18 | 8 |
| 9 | 20 | 9 |
| 10 | 22 | 10 |

"Kids shouldn't be told that there is only one way to do something," Peters states.

# Van Hiele's Levels of Geometric Reasoning

As students' understanding of geometry and geometric proof grows, they progress through levels. A student at level 1 can't understand level 3 without first gaining the understandings at level 2.

**Level 0:** The first level is visual. Students can think about shapes as wholes but not about properties of shapes. For example, they can see that triangles and squares have different numbers of sides, but they don't see how the sizes of their angles matter. Some students enter geometry courses at this level.

**Level 1:** Students can think about properties of shapes but not about how kinds of shapes relate. For example, they can see that rectangles have parallel sides, but they don't grasp how that fact implies that all rectangles are also part of a larger collection of parallelograms.

**Level 2:** Students can think about how kinds of shapes relate well enough to organize them into hierarchies but not well enough to prove properties logically. For example, it may be clear that all rectangles are parallelograms, but it's not clear that *therefore* every rectangle has all the properties of parallelograms, such as point symmetry.

**Level 3:** Students can logically prove properties of kinds of shapes within a logical system.

There's a higher Van Hiele level in which students can critique different logical systems, but this level is generally not relevant to high school geometry.

*Source:* Reprinted with permission. "Van Hiele Levels of Geometric Reasoning," Key Curriculum Press, 1150 65th Street, Emeryville, CA 94608, 1-800-995-MATH, www.keypress.com.

---

**Measurement**

---

▶ Understand measurable attributes of objects and the units, systems, and processes of measurement.

▶ Apply appropriate techniques, tools, and formulas to determine measurements.

Standards are listed with the permission of the National Council of Teachers of Mathematics (NCTM). NCTM does not endorse the content or validity of these alignments.

---

One of the time-honored traditions of childhood involves what may be the first measurement activity a child engages in: How tall am I? Like all good math problems, it's set in a real-world context and the learner has a real motivation to arrive at a result, which is usually etched in pencil on a family room wall.

Cynthia Cliche understands the power of motivation and real-world settings to make learning meaningful—and fun. She recalls that her class embarked on a study about perimeter when one of her students announced in class that his brother was studying the subject: "What is perimeter?" he demanded. "You haven't taught us about perimeter!"

So Cliche began the exploration by asking students to measure the length and width of pieces of pond-shaped felt. Then she posed this question: "If you wanted to go around the pond, how would you measure it?" Cliche posted the students' ponds, complete with cutout fish, on the bulletin board. "Now, of course, perimeter is part of my 1st grade curriculum," she notes.

The project borne of a student's interest (and sibling rivalry) was taken to a new level the following year when a colleague of Cliche's wanted to place stones around the pond on the school grounds. How many stones would he need? "What a perfect lesson," says Cliche, who immediately accepted the assignment for her students. They followed the same process to arrive at a formula for determining perimeter and gave an estimate on the number

# Van Hiele's Levels
## *Implications for Instruction*

The work of two Dutch educators, Pierre van Hiele and Dina van Hiele-Geldof, has given us a vision around which to design geometry curriculum.

Geometry taught in the elementary school should be informal. Such informal geometry activities should be exploratory and hands-on to provide children with the opportunity to investigate, to build and take apart, to create and make drawings, and to make observations about shapes in the world around them. This provides the basis for more formal activities at higher levels.

Teaching a geometry lesson at one van Hiele level when students are functioning at a lower level may hinder student learning. For example, a teacher asks his or her students to play the "What am I?" game with properties of geometric figures, saying, "I have four sides and all of my interior angles are right angles. What am I?" To answer this question, a student must be functioning at Level 2 (analysis) in van Hiele's model of geometric reasoning.

If the students in this class are functioning at Level 1 (visualization), where they recognize a figure by its appearance, they will not be able to play the game. If students are at different levels in one class, the teacher must use differentiated instruction to meet the needs of all of his or her students.

Diagnostic assessment will help to determine the developmental level in geometry for each student. Here are some activities that would be appropriate for students at each level.

1. **Visualization**
   - Sorting, identifying, and describing shapes

   - Manipulating physical models

   - Seeing different sizes and orientations of the same shape as to distinguish characteristics of a shape and the features that are not relevant

   - Building, drawing, making, putting together, and taking apart shapes

2. **Analysis**
   - Shifting from simple identification to properties by using concrete or virtual models to define, measure, observe, and change properties

   - Using models or technology to focus on defining properties, making property lists, and discussing sufficient conditions to define a shape

   - Doing problem solving, including tasks in which properties of shapes are important components

   - Classifying using properties of shapes

3. **Informal Deduction**
   - Doing problem solving, including tasks in which properties of shapes are important components

   - Using models and property lists and discussing which group of properties constitute a necessary and sufficient condition for a specific shape

   - Using informal, deductive language (all, some, none, if-then, what if, and so on)

   - Investigating certain relationships among polygons to establish if the converse is also valid (e.g., If a quadrilateral is a rectangle, it must have four right angles;

if a quadrilateral has four right angles, must it also be a rectangle?)

• Using models and drawings (including dynamic geometry software) as tools to look for generalizations and counter-examples

• Making and testing hypotheses

• Using properties to define a shape or determine if a particular shape is included in a given set

Students usually do not reach Levels 4 and 5 until high school or college, but teachers should be aware of these levels nonetheless.

**4. Deduction.** Students can go beyond just identifying characteristics of shapes and are able to construct proofs using postulates or axioms and definitions. A typical high school geometry course should be taught at this level.

**5. Rigor.** This is the highest level of thought in the van Hiele hierarchy. Students at this level can work in different geometric or axiomatic systems and would most likely be enrolled in a college-level course in geometry.

*Source:* Reprinted/adapted with permission from *Images: A Resource Guide for Improving Measurement and Geometry in Elementary Schools,* by Zimmer, J., Dowshen, A., and Ebersole, D. (2004). Philadelphia, PA: Research for Better Schools.

of stones required. "The students see all the rocks out there and their heads are in the clouds," Cliche says. The students have also earned a new nickname: the pond dwellers.

Preparing a garden plot was the real-world problem for children in Valerie Rose-Piver's 3rd grade class at Hillview Crest Elementary School in Hayward, California. Rose-Piver first read

Barbara Clooney's *Miss Rumphius*, a story about a little girl who wants to travel to far away places. Her grandfather asks her to be sure that she leaves the places she visits more beautiful than when she came (Clooney, 1985).

Rose-Piver asked her students to plan a rectangular-shaped garden with this literary character in mind. Her students first created multiplication arrays for a 24-square-foot garden (students could have four distinct rectangles: 1 x 24; 2 x 12; 3 x 8; and 4 x 6). They then drew diagrams of the arrays on graph paper, cut them out, and labeled them.

A key part of the activity was the debriefing, Rose-Piver states. "We talked about the outcomes and about their decisions," she says. Students had to describe why they thought a particular plot would be most appropriate for Miss Rumphius, who felt she had a responsibility to make the world more beautiful.

---

### Data Analysis and Probability

▶ Formulate questions that can be addressed with data and collect, organize, and display relevant data to answer them.

▶ Select and use appropriate statistical methods to analyze data.

▶ Develop and evaluate inferences and predictions that are based on data.

▶ Understand and apply basic concepts of probability.

Standards are listed with the permission of the National Council of Teachers of Mathematics (NCTM). NCTM does not endorse the content or validity of these alignments.

---

It's a fact of this modern world: students today are inundated with statistical and quantitative information. Information, observes Seeley, "is scrawled across the bottom of the T.V. screen. Students can pick up a newspaper and see quantitative information that they've never seen before." Data is everywhere. Students, as a result, have to become more quantitatively literate, says Seeley.

First graders in Cliche's class begin to analyze data by creating pictorial displays of information about themselves. In the spring, for example, Cliche's students will create colorful egg glyphs. "Students who like their eggs fried will start with a yellow egg; scrambled egg lovers get a pink egg," Cliche explains. Students who like bacon would adorn their yellow or pink eggs with squiggly lines; those who like sausage will decorate their eggs with straight lines. Each child creates a glyph that represents his or her relationship with eggs, and Cliche posts them on the board. As a class, they then analyze the data and create a bar graph that reveals the students' egg preferences.

When Rose-Piver taught 3rd grade (she is now an English language development support teacher at Hillview Crest Elementary School), she helped her students become more discerning consumers by asking them to analyze the accuracy of the data included in the packaging of the products their families purchased. "I've asked children to read a cereal box and think about how they would determine if the advertising about the product was truthful," she says.

*Students in Cynthia Cliche's class design their egg glyphs according to their preferences.*

## Problem Solving

▌ Build new mathematical knowledge through problem solving.

▌ Solve problems that arise in mathematics and in other contexts.

▌ Apply and adapt a variety of appropriate strategies to solve problems.

▌ Monitor and reflect on the process of mathematical problem solving.

Standards are listed with the permission of the National Council of Teachers of Mathematics (NCTM). NCTM does not endorse the content or validity of these alignments.

*Even fairly good students, when they have obtained the solution of the problem and written down neatly the argument, shut their books and look for something else. Doing so, they miss an important and instructive phase of the work. . . .*

*A good teacher should understand and impress on his students
the view that no problem is completely exhausted.* (Pólya,
1985 pp. 14–15)

Many people equate problem solving with using an algorithm
to solve an equation, says Barbara Reys, distinguished professor
of mathematics education at the University of Missouri. "Mention
problem solving and many people will say, 'Oh, I haven't done
a long division problem in years,'" she observes. Division is a
process, says Reys, and it's important that people understand
"when it's an appropriate tool to use."

Of course, understanding division—what it is and when to use
it—is only one of many tools that teachers help students attain.
Students will be presented with many different problems in their
lives, Reys states. The more tools they have, the easier it will be
for them to "reduce a complex situation into something they can
translate, represent, and sort out."

Members of this cell-phone generation, for example, will need
to know how to determine which cell-phone plan best meets their
needs. Rather than just take the first plan they come to, students
should be able to analyze the data to make a well-informed decision, Reys contends. "They can put the information about various
plans in a spreadsheet to compare programs," she says. They can
graph the features of each plan, along with the cost of each, to
identify the best value. The key, Reys suggests, is that students
must be able to determine which strategy or tool will help them
best make sense of the information they have

A respect for various approaches to problem solving is something Cliche hopes to instill in her students. To do so, Cliche will
often pose problems to her 1st graders but not suggest a strategy. For example, she once asked students to work together to

*The more tools
students have, the
easier it will be for
them to reduce a
complex situation into
something they can
translate, represent,
and sort out.*

# Meeting the Process Standards
## *An Interview with Marilyn Burns*

### By Terese Herrera, ENC Instructional Resources

In planning instruction, a teacher needs to look at the content and say, "What is it that I want my children to understand?" and secondly, "What is it that I want them to be able to do with that understanding?" It is really a question of both concepts and skills.

Teachers first need to have a sense of what the content is, and that's outlined in the five content standards. Then the next thing, the question that I always ask myself, is: "What experiences can I provide the children that would give them a way to start to make sense of this for themselves?" This is where I look at the process standards because they really address what children need to do to learn math:

- **Problem solving.** What kinds of problems can I present to children that would give them a chance to grapple with important ideas and skills?

- **Reasoning and proof.** What kinds of situations can I pose to children so that their reasoning is engaged and they have experience giving convincing arguments?

- **Communication.** How do I involve children in talking and writing to help them communicate what they are studying and learning, and hear the ideas of others?

- **Connections.** How do I help children see the connections among mathematical ideas rather than seeing concepts as isolated and separate from one another?

- **Representation.** How do I help children use the symbolism of mathematics to describe their thinking?

> When I am planning new experiences for children, I use those five process standards as my guidelines. I say, "Am I providing kids the opportunity to problem solve, reason/give proof, communicate, connect, and represent?"

*Source:* "An Interview with Marilyn Burns: Meeting the Standards—Don't Try to Do It All by Yourself," by T. Herrera, 2001, *ENC Focus 8*(2), pp. 16–19. Reproduced with permission of Eisenhower National Clearinghouse; visit ENC Online at www.enc.org.

come up with a strategy for addressing this problem: In a 12-hour period, how many times do the combination of digits on a digital clock combine to equal 10?

When the groups shared their strategies after approximately 10 minutes of discussion, the unique ways in which they approached the problem became evident. One group listed number sentences that they eventually converted to a digital display of time: *6 + 4 = 10,* so *6:04* is one combination, and so on. Another group made a model of the digital clock and made time strips—*12:00, 12:01, 12:02, 12:03,* and so on—which they then pulled through their model clock, being careful to note when a number combination equaled 10. The intent of the exercise was to find ways to approach the problem, says Cliche. All strategies, therefore, were appropriate. Students could determine in another lesson which of the approaches was most efficient.

Jennifer Buttars' 2nd grade students have a daily opportunity to exercise their problem-solving skills when they consider the problem of the day. Each problem is different, but the process the class uses is similar so students will understand what to do, Buttars explains. It starts with a story problem, such as: There were 15 cars parked in the lot and 9 parked on the street. How many more cars were parked in the lot? "We read the problem together

# Solving the Problem in Four Steps

In *How to Solve It*, George Pólya describes four steps for solving problems and outlines them at the very beginning of the book for easy reference. The steps outline a series of general questions that allow students to see the problem-solving process on paper. Pólya designed the questions to be general enough that students could apply them to almost any problem.

The four steps are

1. Understanding the problem.

2. Devising a plan.

3. Carrying out the plan.

4. Looking back.

In the first step, students should be able to state the unknown or what they need to find to answer the question; the data the question gives them to work with; and the condition or limiting circumstances they must work around. If they can identify all of these, and explain the question to other people, then they have a good understanding of what the problem is asking. Pólya suggests that students draw a picture if possible or introduce some kind of notation to visualize the question.

To devise a plan, students can start by trying to think of a related problem they have solved before. It may also be helpful for the student to think of a problem they have solved before that had a similar unknown. Students can also try to restate the problem in an easier or different way and try to solve that. By looking at these related problems, students may be able to use the same method or other part of the plan used.

Once students have decided which calculations, computations, or constructions they need and have made sure that all data and conditions were used, they can try out their plan. To carry out the plan, they must do all the calculations and check them as they go along. Then they should ask themselves, "Can I see it is right?" and then, "Can I prove it is right?"

When students look back on the problem and the plan they carried out, they can increase their understanding of the solution. It is always good to recheck the result and argument used and to make sure that it is possible to check them. Then students should ask, "Can I get the result in a different way?" and "Can I use this for another problem?"

*Source:* Adapted from "Pólya's How to Solve It," by B. Nuckolls, 1998. Posted to the *Web of Problem Solving: Problem Solving Island* and retrieved June 15, 2005, at www .math.grin.edu/~rebelsky/ProblemSolving/Essays/polya.html

and then determine what we need to know in order to solve it," she explains.

The discussion that follows students working on the problem is the most important part of the exercise, says Buttars. Just as children need to build their confidence in their ability to solve something and reason through something, they also must learn to respect the reasoning of others. "We have a climate of respect in our classroom," Buttars states. She tells students that "if one of your peers is talking, you need to listen and pay attention." Such an environment gives Buttars and her students "a framework for pulling math out."

The focus on helping children develop their ability to reason helps explain why fewer teachers are using the "key word" approach to teaching problem solving, says Leanne Luttrell. Rather

**Flower Power**
*Sally has 19 tulips in her garden. She also has some daffodils in her garden. She has 50 flowers all together. How many daffodils does she have?*

than teaching students to look for words that suggest a particular operation, teachers instead show students how to analyze a problem "to truly understand what is being asked," she states.

Students' understanding is bolstered when they analyze a mathematical situation quantitatively, write Lisa Clement and Jamal Bernhard in "A Problem-Solving Alternative to Using Key Words." This includes asking

- What quantities are involved in this situation?

- What quantities am I trying to find?

- Which quantities are critical to the problem at hand?

- Are any of these quantities related to each other? If so, how?

- Do I know the values of any of the quantities? If so, which ones? (2005, p. 364)

Students can also create a diagram that helps them visualize the problem, Clement and Bernhard note. Approaching problem solving keeps the focus on "making sense of mathematical situations" (p. 365).

### Reasoning and Proof

▶ Recognize reasoning and proof as fundamental aspects of mathematics.
▶ Make and investigate mathematical conjectures.
▶ Develop and evaluate mathematical arguments and proofs.
▶ Select and use various types of reasoning and methods of proof.

Standards are listed with the permission of the National Council of Teachers of Mathematics (NCTM). NCTM does not endorse the content or validity of these alignments.

"If problem solving is the focus of mathematics, reasoning is the logical thinking that helps us decide if and why our answers make sense," writes John Van de Walle in *Elementary and Middle School Mathematics: Teaching Developmentally* (5th edition; 2004, p. 4). And, Van de Walle continues, if students think their answers make sense, they must also develop the ability to defend their reasoning (2004). In defending their reasoning and giving a rationale for their responses, students also deepen their own understanding of mathematical concepts or ideas.

Leanne Luttrell makes sure her 4th and 5th grade students have many reasoning and proof activities, and her students soon learn that she won't give them the answers. Luttrell firmly believes that people have to discover for themselves the mathematical concepts and formulas that were proven long ago. She won't provide formulas. "Anyone can put numbers into a formula, but they need to understand why formulas are true and why equations work," says Luttrell.

To help them develop a formula for the area of a triangle, for example, Luttrell gave her students geoboards and asked them to copy sample triangles onto the boards. Using their knowledge of the area of rectangles ($A = length \times width$), students were asked to find the area of a triangle by studying right, acute, and obtuse triangles. Will they need to use more than one rectangle? Students knew a diagonal connecting opposite corners of a rectangle divides the rectangle in half, but they had to recall and apply this knowledge. Luttrell then prompted students to find patterns in their work. Based on their work, can they determine a formula for finding the area of triangles? Will their formula work for all types of triangles? Why or why not?

This one or two-day activity is powerful when students begin to see the formula, says Luttrell. The real learning occurs, however, when students "explain to their peers how they would find the area of a triangle."

Mistakes are no longer feared in today's mathematics classroom; indeed, they're celebrated, say educators. A student's error can lead to rich discussions about why a certain approach to a learning issue did or didn't work. In today's classrooms, you'll find "mathematics communities," writes Van de Walle (2004, p. 6). Students can share their thinking without fear of ridicule, state many of the teachers interviewed for this book. And in that willingness to communicate, students find new ways to understand math.

---

### Communication

▶ Organize and consolidate mathematical thinking though communication.

▶ Communicate mathematical thinking coherently and clearly to peers, teachers, and others.

▶ Analyze and evaluate the mathematical thinking and strategies of others.

▶ Use the language of mathematics to express mathematical ideas precisely.

Standards are listed with the permission of the National Council of Teachers of Mathematics (NCTM). NCTM does not endorse the content or validity of these alignments.

---

*I'm sorry to say that the subject I most disliked was mathematics. I have thought about it. I think the reason was that mathematics leaves no room for argument. If you made a mistake, that was all there was to it.*
*—Malcom X*

"We really work on that communication piece," says Francine Plotycia, whose favorite question is, Does your answer make sense? Her 2nd grade students are accustomed to hearing her say, "Explain to us how you did that." Plotycia also emphasizes public speaking. "The ability to articulate clearly is a wonderful life skill," she states.

Making thinking visible is an important part of communication, says LeeAnn Cervini, the K–5 enrichment specialist at Terry A. Taylor Elementary School in Spencerport, New York. When she taught 1st grade, Cervini would ask her students to share how they problem solve and arrive at a solution. What she hoped is that "light bulbs would turn on in other students' heads."

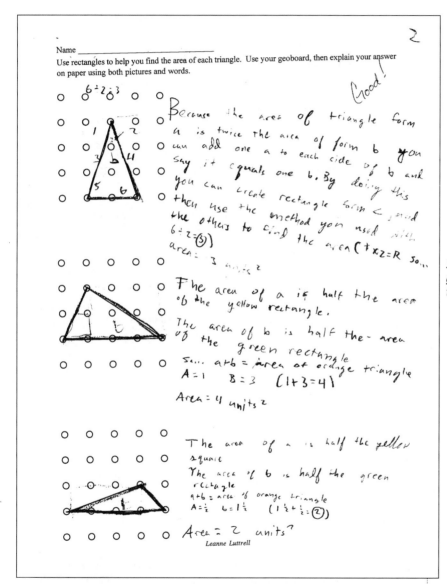

2

Name _____

Use rectangles to help you find the area of each triangle. Use your geoboard, then explain your answer on paper using both pictures and words.

Good!

Because the area of triangle form a is twice the area of form b you can add one a to each side of b and say it equals one b. By doing this you can create rectangle form c and then use the method you used with the others to find the area ( † x 2 = R so... 6 ÷ 2 = (3))

area: 3 units²

The area of a is half the area of the yellow rectangle.

The area of b is half the area of the green rectangle

So... a + b = area of orange triangle
A = 1   B = 3   (1 + 3 = 4)

Area = 4 units²

The area of a is half the yellow square

The area of b is half the green rectangle

a + b = area of orange triangle
A = ½   b = 1½   (1½ + ½ = (2))

Area = 2 units²

Leanne Luttrell

*Students used geoboards to discover the arc of triangles.*

Cervini, who has a master's degree in literacy, finds that walking through a problem-solving process aloud helps students see how we, "come to an 'ah ha' in our thinking." It's important for students and the teacher to model that thinking process because it helps students make connections, she says.

Frequent questioning is a technique Ashley Berk employs to foster communication among her 5th graders. "I present a lot of open-ended questions for them to struggle with and discuss together," she says. Such conversations help to build "a nice community where kids are comfortable taking risks." Her students, Berk adds, "are very comfortable saying, 'I don't understand.'"

---

### Connections

▶ Recognize and use connections among mathematical ideas.

▶ Understand how mathematical ideas interconnect and build on one another to produce a coherent whole.

▶ Recognize and apply mathematics in contexts outside of mathematics.

Standards are listed with the permission of the National Council of Teachers of Mathematics (NCTM). NCTM does not endorse the content or validity of these alignments.

---

If Linda Figgins has her way, her students will never experience mathematics as something separate from other subjects—or life. "My students don't even know they're doing math," says Figgins, a 6th grade teacher at McKinley Elementary School in Elgin, Illinois. "When a reporter asked whether a lesson we were doing was math or science, they replied, 'Well, it's both.'"

That seamlessness can be achieved when lesson activities are built around real-world problems. A lesson called Justin's Garden (adapted from *Connected Math*) was designed to give students practice in working with fractions, decimals, and percentages while giving them ideas on how they can harvest fresh vegetables in their urban setting.

"I tell students that Dad has a city plot of 100 square meters and he wants to plant a garden," Figgins explains. The students must then divide the plot among several vegetables. There are a number of possible solutions, and students are encouraged to be creative, but Figgins reminds them that Dad wants

- Twice as many tomatoes as potatoes.

- At least one row of cucumbers.

- Room for carrots, eggplant, and radishes.

With these criteria, students divided the 100 meters accordingly. "We then decided to plant the garden in a terrarium, so we had to scale it down," says Figgins. Students had only 10 squares. "How can you create a smaller version of Justin's garden using the same criteria?" she asks her students.

Helping students develop a number sense while also honing a life skill was the impetus behind Cervini's in-class banking system. "I developed the lesson over nine years in teaching 1st grade," she explains. It started as a behavior modification technique in which the children were awarded "smart tickets" for modeling appropriate behavior; children could use the smart tickets to purchase a small token at the end of the week.

Cervini then realized that the system could be used to help children learn the number system. "I tweaked the exercise just a bit and began awarding play money instead of tickets," she says. Students would receive money every day, all year long. Once a week, students would have to use the number system to sort the money they collected into piles of ones, tens, and hundreds. Once students had sorted their cash, they would write equations that represented the amounts they had in each column ($3 + 20 + 200 = \underline{\hspace{1em}}$, for example).

The ongoing activity was highly motivating, Cervini notes. Students enjoyed counting their money and recording the amount in their savings books. Students could then spend their play money on old McDonald's toys, stuffed animals, books, cards, pencils, stickers, and so on. "I had a basket for $50 items, as well as one with $500 items, so if a child wanted an expensive stuffed toy, he'd have to save for it," she says.

At the end of the year, children could buy ice cream and many chose to save for the expensive treat. Cervini remembers one 1st grade boy who decided he wanted to buy all his classmates ice cream. "He saved his money and by end of the year, he was able to figure out what it would cost to buy each person ice cream. The total was $9,000, and he was so proud of himself." That little boy is in 5th grade now and is well liked. "He's one of our school leaders," says Cervini.

---

### Representation

▶ Create and use representations to organize, record, and communicate mathematical ideas.

▶ Select, apply, and translate among mathematical representations to solve problems;

▶ Use representations to model and interpret physical, social, and mathematical phenomena.

Standards are listed with the permission of the National Council of Teachers of Mathematics (NCTM). NCTM does not endorse the content or validity of these alignments.

---

As a mathematics teacher, Luttrell has become adept at drawing lesson activities from many sources—from published curricula, the textbook, and her own mathematical knowledge base. She, no doubt, can find many ways of teaching one concept. That ability to see connections between different interpretations of an idea and to understand how they relate can then be turned around: she can represent a mathematical idea or data in different ways.

Luttrell knows that she must help her students become equally as dexterous in their mathematical thinking. Lately, she has considered how she might incorporate an idea from the *Singapore*

*Math* curricula: students draw pictures to represent variables in an algebraic expression, "but they don't know that that's what it is at that point," she says. "It's amazing how well that picture ties in with the algebra that you would use on an abstract level."

Such visual representations help make numbers real for students, says Mary Short. To help her 2nd graders understand how different denominations of money can represent the same amount, she first read *A Chair for My Mother* by Vera B. Williams. After a fire destroys their home, the characters in the book save dimes and nickels until they can afford to buy a big comfortable chair. Short then brought in some coins—quarters, dimes, and nickels—and asked students to draw pictures that show the worth of each. She asked students: How many quarters would I need for $10? How many dimes would I need for $10? How many nickels?

"I then took the visual representation exercise a step further," says Short. She and the students worked together to create a chart showing that one dime is equal to two nickels, that one nickel and five pennies is also equal to the value of a dime, and that ten pennies is equal to the value of one dime, and so on, for each of the coins.

In addition to charts, representations can include diagrams, graphical displays, and symbolic expressions. Luttrell likes to challenge her students with logic puzzles. In an activity she wrote for her book *Perplexing Logic Puzzles Using Venn Diagrams*, for example, Luttrell asks students to determine how many students were surveyed while volunteering in their community. She provided the following clues.

Several elementary students were volunteering in their community. Students were asked if they had helped collect food for the hungry, collect toys for hospitalized children, or cleaned the park. Survey results revealed

• Forty-one people helped clean the park.

• Fifty-one people helped collect food.

• Forty-four people helped collect toys.

• Only one student did all three activities.

• Seventeen people collected food and toys but did not clean the park.

• Twelve people helped collect toys and clean the park but did not collect food.

• Forty-three people participated in more than one activity.

• Seven people surveyed had not volunteered.

The problem then required that students determine how many students were surveyed.

To work on this problem, students first had to label each of the eight sections of their three-circle Venn diagrams with A, B, C, D, and so on. Then, students could plug in the data from the clues: $A + B + D + E = 51$ is one expression for those who collected food, for example; $D + E + F + G = 41$ is an expression for the number of people who helped clean the park, and so on. Luttrell provided just enough information to allow students to immediately plug numbers in for some of the variables, which then allowed them to find the value of the "mystery" variables.

These kinds of activities are challenging, says Luttrell. More importantly, perhaps, is that the puzzles give students opportunities to see the different ways a number can be represented. What's more, these activities can "increase my students' ability to perceive and define relationships and organize information," she states.

**Volunteers**

collect food             collect toys

A  B  C

E

D  F    H

G

clean the park

clue 1: D+E+F+G=41
clue 2: A+B+D+E=51
clue 3: B+C+E+F=44
clue 4: E=1
clue 5: B=17
clue 6: F=12
clue 7: B+D+E+F=43; 17+D+1+12=43
       so D=13
       *(from clue 1)  13+1+12+G=41
       so G=15
       *(from clue 2)  A+17+13+1=51
       so A=20
       *(from clue 3)  17+C+1+12=44
       so C=14
clue 8: H=7

A= 20
B= 17
C= 14
D= 13
E=  1
F= 12
G= 15
H=  7

A+B+C+D+E+F+G+H= 99

Ninety-nine students completed the survey.

*Students plugged in data from the clues to find the values of the "mystery" variables.*

# Assessment That Serves Instruction

*Assessment comes from the Latin root which means "to sit." And when we talk about assessment in the classroom, we're talking about sitting with the student's work. And that idea of sitting with the work and seeing what it says about that student is what assessment is about.*

*It's different from evaluation, which is then giving a certain value to that work. That is when I have to name it a C or number it a 75. And the two acts are quite separate and have different purposes in the classroom. The purpose of assessment is ultimately to help students with their work.*

—*Steven Levy in* Using Classroom Assessment
to Guide Daily Instruction

Educators agree that assessment—classroom assessment, that is—is integral to teaching: what teachers learn about students' understanding helps them determine the direction of their instruction.

"Assessment cannot be viewed as this 'big test,'" asserts Seeley. Assessment must be used "to help teachers see, on an ongoing basis, what their students know so we can catch problems early, so we can guide student learning."

Students are better served when teachers have embraced this view of assessment, agrees Thomas P. Carpenter, emeritus professor of curriculum and instruction at the University of Wisconsin–Madison. Teachers need to "assess their students' ability to engage in practices *while* [emphasis added] they are engaged in those practices," he says. In other words, the best way to determine if students can problem solve is to watch them as they solve a problem.

In classrooms where "teachers are constantly observing what students are doing as they are doing it," the goal is on building understanding, Carpenter states. In these classrooms, conversations about the math are key, and teachers require that students explain and justify their answers. And, research shows that students in these classrooms do every bit as well on standardized tests, Carpenter says.

Those standardized tests have attained a greater prominence in the minds of teachers today, however. All teachers want to help their students achieve a deep understanding of mathematical concepts, but many must also contend with accountability mandates set by their schools, districts, and states.

"Standardized testing is often a separate activity from the daily assessment that occurs in teachers' classrooms," write Wendy B. Sanchez and Nicole F. Ice in "Strike a Balance in Assessment" (2005, para. 1). They note that classroom assessment and standardized assessment have different purposes. Still, write Sanchez and Ice, the "goal of all assessment is to maximize students' success" (2005, para. 2). The authors call for an alignment between measures: "Although standardized assessment is not necessarily used to guide teaching, thoughtful use of classroom assessment methods can promote learning that will enable students to understand mathematics and perform well on standardized assessments," Sanchez and Ice maintain (2005, para. 2).

> ## Know Your Terms
>
> ### Formative Assessments
>
> - Used to diagnose what students have learned to plan further instruction.
> - Occur when teachers feed information back to students in ways that enable the student to learn better.
> - Encourage students to engage in a similar, self-reflective process.
>
> ---
>
> *Source:* Adapted from "The Value of Formatiave Assessment," 1999, *FairTest Examiner.* Retrieved October 12, 2005, from www.fairtest.org/examarts/winter99/k-forma3.html

Buttars believes she maintains a nice balance in her classroom. Because her students are 2nd graders, she relies primarily on informal assessment—not a lot of homework or many unit tests, she says. Still, "over the course of a week, I make sure I get around and check in with every student's progress. I keep anecdotal notes, and if I see a lot of students making the same error, I'll work that into the next day's problem."

Still, she is aware that her students will have to take the state criterion-referenced test, so she makes a game of helping them become more familiar with the format of a standardized test. "I try

## Helping Teachers Learn About Assessment

Assessment is the NCTM Professional Development Focus of the Year for the 2005–06 school year. Throughout the year, NCTM will publish articles that relate to assessment in the association's print publications and on its Web site (look for a magnifying glass icon); there will also be assessment-related sessions at NCTM conferences and meetings.

All the Focus of the Year resources and activities will reflect the NCTM's Assessment Principle:

*Assessment should support the learning of important mathematics and furnish useful information to both teachers and students.*

Assessment should be more than merely a test at the end of instruction to gauge learning. It should be an integral part of instruction that guides teachers and enhances students' learning.

Teachers should be continually gathering information about their students through questions, interviews, writing tasks, and other means. They can then make appropriate decisions about such matters as reviewing material, reteaching a difficult concept, or providing something more or different for students who are struggling or need enrichment.

To be consistent with the Learning Principle, assessments should focus on understanding as well as procedural skills. Because different students show what they know and can do in different ways, assessments should also be done in multiple ways, and teachers should look for a convergence of evidence from different sources.

Teachers must ensure that all students are given an opportunity to demonstrate their mathematics learning. For example, teachers should use communication-enhancing and bilingual techniques to support students who are learning English.

to make it fun," says Buttars. "I might ask students, Which one of these answers did they put in there to trick you? What would happen if you didn't read that word correctly? I want them to think through the questions." Her students know that the standardized test is a "big deal," but Buttars doesn't want them to be afraid of taking it. And giving her students exposure to the kinds of questions that are on the test has helped—Buttars' students have performed well compared with district averages.

In the Abingdon, Maryland, school district, the tie between state assessments and curriculum and instruction is a bit more formal. As a result, Plotycia plans her lessons to address those assessments and teaches her 2nd graders the skills they'll need to be successful on the district-level test. If three-digit addition and subtraction is on the test, for example, Plotycia will give her students plenty of practice doing those

## Know Your Terms

### Diagnostic Assessment

- Conducting a formal diagnostic assessment means that the teacher uses a carefully constructed evaluation instrument to gather information about a student's current level of achievement.

- Formal diagnostic instruments take time to create, administer, and review.

- A formal diagnostic assessment, when done well, provides accurate information about a student's academic achievement. The assessment can also help teachers assess a student's readiness to learn new content.

*Source:* Adapted from *How to Change to a Nongraded School,* M. Hunter, 1992. Alexandria, VA: Association for Supervision and Curriculum Development.

procedures in class. As a result, students don't fear the end-of-unit assessment, she says.

And, yet, classroom assessment remains a large part of Plotycia's instruction. "I assess learning in so many different ways," she says. "I use a checklist and observe. If I can see that they've mastered a particular skill, I'll check it off. My students write journal entries. And I also conduct mini-interviews with students during independent work time." Through these daily classroom interactions, Plotycia knows what to teach next.

*Assessment is communication. It can be as simple as asking, Where are the kids? Where should I go now?*

"Assessment is communication," says Mark Saul, a program manager at the National Science Foundation and veteran New York teacher. "It can be as simple as asking yourself, 'Where are the kids, where should I go now?'"

"The important thing is for teachers to ask: 'Now that I know this about my student, what do I do tomorrow?'" agrees John Holloway, a researcher for the Educational Testing Service.

Many teachers have also started asking a new question, What does the data suggest I do next? "The environment has become so much more quantitative; data becomes more and more important," observes Jim Bohan, the K–12 mathematics program coordinator in the Manheim Township School District in Lancaster, Pennsylvania. His district, in response, has established action-research teams that will gauge the effectiveness of the elementary math program. "We're really

## Know Your Terms

### Summative Assessments

- Attempt to summarize student learning at some point—at the end of a course, for example.
- Are not designed to provide the kind of feedback that guides instruction during the learning process.
- Can guide school administrators in deciding what learning opportunities will be offered to students.
- Can guide teachers in determining how to organize their courses.

Most standardized tests are summative.

*Source:* From "The Value of Formatiave Assessment," 1999, FairTest Examiner. Retrieved October 12, 2005, from www .fairtest.org/examarts/winter99/k-forma3.html

excited about this," Bohan states, because building in a data-driven component will help teachers and administrators identify where the alignment between state and district standards and classroom instruction needs to be adjusted, he suggests.

## Involving Students in the Assessment Process

Teacher-constructed assessments can provide important information about student learning, but students can also reflect on and evaluate their own learning, which provides rich information for teachers, say experts.

Learning is not a spectator sport, Kathleen Fitzpatrick told educators at the ASCD 2002 Teaching and Learning Conference. How can educators ensure that students take an active role? One way is to emphasize self-assessment. Have students put into their own words what standards and performance criteria mean, Fitzpatrick advised. "When students can tell me what a learning standard is about, it's a strong indicator [that learning is] real to kids" (2002).

"I have never met anyone who plans on failure," writes Betty McDonald in "Self-Assessment for Student Success" (2004, p. 4). "Every student I have met plans on succeeding academically and in life and is happy to embrace strategies that lead to that success. Teaching students to assess their own work is one of those strategies," she writes (see Tom's Story, p. 103).

"As you plan for a self-assessment, consider how you want the assessment to help you as a teacher," writes John Van de Walle in *Elementary and Middle School Mathematics: Teaching Developmentally*. Remember, he writes, students' self-assessments are "not your measure of their learning or disposition, but rather a record of how *they perceive* these things" (2004, p. 71).

## Future Focus

Research-based . . . Data-driven . . . these are two phrases that have gained a foothold in education-speak. The time may be right to create a new, district-level position to support the efforts that result when these two phrases are enacted.

"Maybe what's needed now is a director of research and assessment," suggests John Holloway, a researcher for the Educational Testing Service. School leaders need to ensure "that the research that goes into the classroom is practical for teachers," he asserts. The person in this position would "help teachers think about collecting more useful data about their students on a more frequent basis," he says.

According to Holloway, a person in the position he envisions could also "guide people to become aware of new research about what works for different groups of students." For example, are there instructional strategies that are more effective in boosting the math achievement of Hispanic or Asian students? The director of research and assessment would know that, he says.

To gather self-assessment data, Van de Walle suggests giving students

• Some form of questionnaire that may include open-ended questions or limited response choices (seldom, sometimes, often).

## Tom's Story
### *Self-Assessment in Practice*

Tom feels as though he is left out in his math class. He finds it a challenge to concentrate and do well, and he is scared to share his frustrations with his peers for fear of being publicly ridiculed. What options does Tom have? Tom's conscientious teacher, Mr. Ron, recognizes Tom's dilemma and skillfully walks Tom through a self-assessment process that can help Tom fully grasp the challenging concepts of the lesson.

For example, suppose the lesson focuses on sets and Tom must create a symbolic expression for the following diagram:

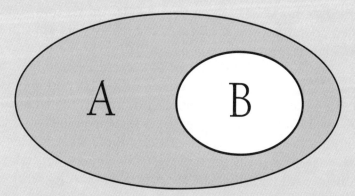

Mr. Ron asks Tom a series of prompting questions that help him focus and recall what he has studied. Did Tom, Mr. Ron asks,

- Discuss this question with anyone?

- Make a checklist of his thoughts?

- Make a mental picture of the diagram?

- Ask himself any questions?

- Look at several texts?

- Review his notes?

- Recall what was discussed in class?

- Think about real-life examples?

- Try making the ideas into a game or song?

- Leave it for a while and then try again?

- Try writing a similar question?

Because Mr. Ron walks him through his own thoughts and ideas, Tom is able to write the correct symbolic expression. Mr. Ron reviews what Tom has done and invites him to articulate his feelings about the exercise. On his own, Tom then does three similar exercises and assesses his work [*see Students' Self-Assessment schedule, p. 105*].

Tom now feels empowered to succeed because he can make his own independent judgments about his work and set about finding ways to improve his performance. Tom understands that his academic progress is his responsibility—and he possesses the tools he needs to achieve success. Tom's self-concept, self-efficacy, and creativity improve noticeably. Absenteeism, tardiness, procrastination, and excuses become practices of the past.

When teachers believe in the potential of their students and use self-assessment skills to empower them, students start to see school as a friendly, hospitable place that fosters learning in a safe atmosphere. More important, they start to see themselves as individuals with unique abilities and talents that can be nurtured and matured for maximum benefit. In other words, they take charge of their learning.

### Students' Self-Assessment Schedule

When students examine their work, they should refer to criteria they've developed with their peers and the teacher. Tom used the following scale to assess three exercises that tested his understanding of sets.

| Exercise done | Mark out of 10 points | Do I think my score met the standard? | My comments or judgments based on the given 10-point score scale |
|---|---|---|---|
| | | Yes (✓) No (✓) | |
| 1 | 2 | ✓ | Poor—I needed to review my notes before doing the exercise. |
| 2 | 7 | ✓ | Good—I understand the concept but was still a little uncertain about which symbol to use. In fact, I guessed. |
| 3 | 10 | ✓ | Excellent—I immediately understood from the diagram what the expression should be and what symbol to use. |

| Score Scale | Judgment |
|---|---|
| 9–10 | Excellent |
| 7–8 | Good |
| 5–6 | Fair |
| 0–4 | Poor |

*Source:* From "Self-Assessment for Student Success," by B. McDonald, 2004, *Classroom Leadership,* 8(1), pp. 4–5.

• Open-ended writing prompts, such as, How well do you think you understand the work we've been doing on fractions?

• Attitude inventories that allow students to respond with a "yes," "no," or "sometimes" to statements such as, I feel sure of myself when I get an answer to a problem, or, I'm not as good in math as most other students in this class. (Van de Walle, 2004)

No matter what kind of instrument teachers use, Van de Walle states that teachers should give students room to add their own comments at the end of the assessment (2004).

Helping students become reflective about their mathematical understanding begins with asking questions, writes Cindy Hansford in "Using Math to Teach Thinking" (2004). Hansford regularly asks her students, What's the purpose? How did you solve that? Is there a more efficient way? Teachers often begin the practice, she says, but "students soon start asking themselves these questions on a regular basis" (p. 2).

By helping students become reflective, Hansford believes she is helping them "activate their higher-order thinking and reasoning skills" (p. 8). Hansford, a 3rd grade teacher at Meadow View Elementary School in Helena, Alabama, also believes she must give her students opportunities to make decisions in class. "Will they make poor choices? Of course. Everyone does. But, they will also be prepared to evaluate their own thinking to determine if a better solution is possible. Children with this capacity will be the competent and competitive leaders of tomorrow" (2004, p. 8).

## Reflections   ◆ ◆ ◆

In the classrooms of innovative teachers, you'll find students who are active, enthusiastic, and genuinely excited to be discovering the world of mathematics. These innovative teachers have several things in common, including that they

• **Share their effective lessons.** Hundreds—make that thousands—of engaging and effective standards-based lesson plans can be found online. Start with *Illuminations* (http://illuminations.nctm.org), which is a partnership between the National Council of Teachers of Mathematics and MarcoPolo.

• **Understand assessment.** Effective teachers know how assessment is used—both in the classroom and in other contexts. These teachers know the terms that describe assessment practices. And, just as they do for lesson planning, they often look to their peers for examples of assessments they can used to help their children learn.

• **Know that "wrong" answers can provide the right information.** In understanding the various uses of assessment, effective teachers of mathematics now welcome the incorrect response because such responses provide them with invaluable information about how to adjust their instruction.

# What We Believe

The fair and proper use of assessment has long been on the minds of ASCD members, who have consistently approved of the Association's position statements on the practice (in 1971, 1975, 1979, 1987, 1990, 1998):

> *ASCD believes that assessment is valuable when educators use it to guide programs, determine instruction, influence resource allocations, and authentically make judgments about student learning.*

> *Assessments might include norm- or criterion-referenced tests and performance tasks to evaluate students, schools, and programs. Assessments need to clearly reflect curriculum goals, and their use should be guided by the involvement of all those affected by or who have a stake in the assessment process. The general public also needs to be fully engaged in the purposes and uses of assessment data.*

In 2001 and 2004, ASCD members clarified the Associations position on assessment and high-stakes testing, issuing this position statement:

> *Decision makers in education—students, parents, educators, community members, and policymakers— all need timely access to information from many sources. Judgments about student learning and*

education program success need to be informed by multiple measures. Using a single achievement test to sanction students, educators, schools, districts, states/provinces, or countries is an inappropriate use of assessment. ASCD supports the use of multiple measures in assessment systems that are

- Fair, balanced, and grounded in the art and science of learning and teaching;

- Reflective of curricular and developmental goals and representative of content that students have had an opportunity to learn;

- Used to inform and improve instruction;

- Designed to accommodate nonnative speakers and special needs students; and

- Valid, reliable, and supported by professional, scientific, and ethical standards designed to fairly assess the unique and diverse abilities and knowledge base of all students.

*Source:* Adapted from *What We Believe: Positions of the Association for Supervision and Curriculum Development.* Retrieved June 15, 2005, from www.ascd.org

4

# Nurturing Positive
# Attitudes About Math

*It is not enough to have a good mind.*
*The main thing is to use it well.*

—*Descartes*, Discours de la Méthode

When she was in elementary and middle school, Valerie Rose-Piver loved her math classes, but that all changed in high school. "I spiraled down," she recalls. "Algebra was terrible—I took it twice—geometry was worse." Rose-Piver was well into college before she would again venture into a mathematics classroom, and it wasn't until she became a teacher that she discovered a new competence in the subject: Rose-Piver's principal sent her to a two-day math institute, and she was transformed. The enthusiasm that the institute's staff conveyed about mathematics "just rubbed off," she explains. Indeed, says Rose-Piver, a 3rd grade teacher at Hillview Crest Elementary School in Hayward, California, "I remember thinking, 'If this is what math is all about, thank goodness I found it.'"

*Many teachers who come to love mathematics do so after they enter the classroom.*

Rose-Piver's story is echoed by many of the award-winning teachers interviewed for this book. Many of these teachers came to love mathematics—and become great teachers of the subject—only after entering the classroom. With their students, they explore concepts by using manipulatives and work on problems that are connected to the real world. Many of these teachers also, for the first time, experience what it is like to be part of a math community, a place in which everyone works together in pursuit of building an understanding of mathematics.

"I was math phobic" says Francine Plotycia, a 2nd grade teacher at Abingdon Elementary School in Abingdon, Maryland. "I really didn't want to take all those math courses [in college] because I just didn't understand what the professor was doing, so I didn't enjoy graduate-level algebra or geometry at all," she says. What Plotycia did enjoy, however, was the math she did with her students because it made sense to her.

That young people become turned off to mathematics comes as no surprise to Harvey F. Silver and Richard W. Strong, who suggest that teachers too often fail to recognize that "different students have different learning styles and need different things from their math teacher" (Silver & Strong, 2003, p. 6).

Cathy Seeley, president of the NCTM, agrees. The traditional lecture approach that many math teachers employ benefits only some students, she stated in an online discussion with math educators from around the world. "We have seen enough examples to know that some of our students whom we have believed could not learn turn out to be strong math students, sometimes even gifted students, when given the opportunity, resources, expectations and support to learn. When we commit to more student engagement in our teaching, we enable far more students to excel," she says (2005, para. 17).

And enabling more students to excel in mathematics is an imperative, say many educators. In this era of No Child Left Behind and in view of the growing awareness that mathematics knowledge can open doors to continued education and greater earnings, there is an earnest effort to ensure that the same expectations for achievement in mathematics are held for all students. This effort requires that teachers learn how to continually challenge and motivate students who easily comprehend mathematical concepts while meeting the needs of students who struggle with math, especially in the early years when attitudes about the subject are formed.

## Building Mathematical Communities

Nothing kills enthusiasm faster than ridicule. Beth Peters knows this, which is why she makes it a priority to establish community and cooperation in her classroom. The 3rd grade teacher at Village East Elementary School in Aurora, Colorado, knows that no learning—of mathematics or anything else—will take place if her students don't feel free to talk about what they do or don't understand with their teacher and their peers.

*These two students found that, among other things, they both like pizza and math.*

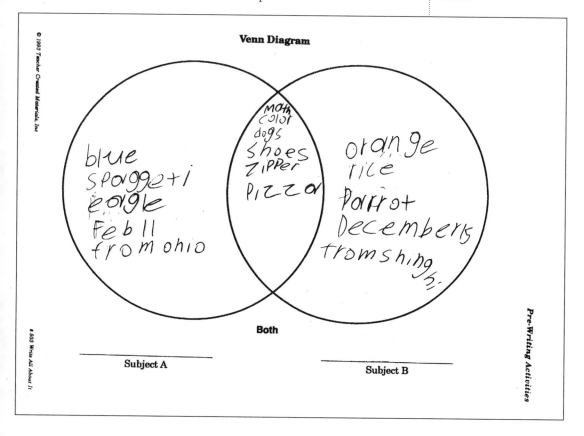

**Venn Diagram**

blue
spaggeti
eagle
Feb 11
from ohio

math
color
dogs
shoes
zipper
pizza

orange
rice
Parrot
December
trom shing

**Both**

_____
Subject A

_____
Subject B

© 1993 Teacher Created Materials, Inc

# 503 Write All About It

Pre-Writing Activities

"At first students would laugh if a peer made a mistake. I had to help them understand that mistakes are not something to be ashamed of—or scoffed at," she says. So, as a first step toward building unity in her classroom, Peters asked her students to create Venn diagrams that mapped out their likenesses and differences. She also asked her students to start "thinking aloud" and explain their reasoning. It was more than a few months before children truly became more respectful toward each other, Peters recalls, but her efforts to strengthen students' interpersonal relationships helped to create an environment in which students felt safe enough to learn from each other.

"We have to build trust," agrees Gail Underwood, a 2nd grade teacher at Grant Elementary School in Columbia, Missouri. At the beginning of the school year, she sets ground rules with her students, telling them, "We're not going to laugh at answers and we're not going to allow others to laugh." After about two months, says Underwood, students have become comfortable with sharing any struggles they might be having. "You'll start to hear students say, 'This is what I'm thinking. I've got two answers, but I'm not sure which one is right, so I'm bringing it to the community.'"

The community to which students refer meets during the daily Math Congress. Students can post on the board "all the answers we get during an investigation," says Underwood. She and her students will then "look at the answers and talk about reasonableness—which of the responses are close?" In sharing answers—even those that are incorrect—Underwood helps her students see themselves "as people who make mistakes but through discussion, can clarify their thinking."

The Math Congress also helps Underwood clarify her instruction. "Sometimes students will share a good strategy or good model—sometimes one I hadn't thought of—and I'll say, 'I want everyone to try Lucy's model today and then check it with yours.' Lucy's model may be a level of sophistication I want them to get to," she explains. Because Underwood regularly points to students' work as models, students don't feel uncomfortable about being singled out; rather, they consider sharing their strategies to be an obligation.

And, by acknowledging that she, the teacher, doesn't have all the answers, the Math Congress ensures that the focus is on learning—not on who is right and who is wrong or who is the authority. As a result, Underwood notes that her students see her as a learner, as someone who is "just a person participating in the Congress." Indeed, says Underwood, students will sometimes "take chalk out of my hand and head to the board." When students display such enthusiasm and are willing to converse about mathematics in a meaningful way, she says, a teacher knows that students are really learning.

## Respecting Diversity Through Differentiated Instruction

Many educators agree that building a sense of community in the classroom lays the foundation for helping students appreciate and accept that they learn in different ways and have different strengths and weaknesses and that how their teacher works with them should reflect a respect for their diversity.

Sometimes a mathematical activity can help drive home that point. One classroom featured in the ASCD video program, *Differentiating Instruction: Instructional and Management Strategies, Tape 2*, shows children beginning to consider the concept of differentiated instruction by identifying their readiness levels in several activities and then graphing their results. The teacher in the

*When students are part of a math community, the focus is on learning, not on who is right and who is wrong or who is the authority.*

# Meeting Individual Needs
# Through Differentiated Instruction

### By Scott Willis and Larry Mann

Nearly all teachers believe that it's better to differentiate instruction—that is, to gear instruction to better meet students' varying readiness levels, learning preferences, and interests. The challenge lies in translating that belief into action.

Carol Ann Tomlinson, an associate professor at the University of Virginia and author of several ASCD books on differentiated instruction, states that teachers can differentiate three aspects of the curriculum: content, process, and products.

**Content** refers to the concepts, principles, and skills that teachers want students to learn. All students should be given access to the same core content, Tomlinson believes. Struggling learners should be taught the same big ideas as their classmates, not given watered-down content.

"Teachers should address the same concepts with all students but adjust the degree of complexity," Tomlinson emphasizes. "The same concept can be explained in a way that's comprehensible to a very young child or in a way that challenges a Ph.D. candidate." To illustrate this point, she cites the example of a professor whom she observed teaching Shakespearean sonnets—with great success—to 1st graders.

Content also refers to the means teachers use to give students access to skills and knowledge, such as texts, lectures, demonstrations, and field trips. Teachers can vary these vehicles as well, Tomlinson says. For example, a teacher might direct an advanced learner to complex texts, Web sites, and experts to interview, while providing a student of more modest capacity with reading buddies, videos, demonstrations, and "organizers that distill information and make it more accessible."

**Process** refers to the activities that help students make sense of, and come to own, the ideas and skills being taught. Teachers can modify these activities, Tomlinson advises, to provide some students with more complexity and others with more scaffolding, depending on their readiness levels. (Examples of scaffolding include step-by-step directions, reteaching, and additional models.) Like content, process can be varied by student interest and learning preferences as well.

**Products** refers to culminating projects that allow students to demonstrate and extend what they have learned. Products reveal whether students can apply learning beyond the classroom to solve problems and take action. Different students can create different products, Tomlinson suggests, based on their readiness levels, interests, and learning preferences. For example, some students might work alone on a product, while others might work in groups.

*Source*: From "Differentiating Instruction: Finding Manageable Ways to Meet Individual Needs," by S. Willis, & L. Mann, 2000, *Curriculum Update*.

featured classroom uses the activity to illustrate the concept of fairness, telling her students that they aren't all doing the same thing because, to be fair, she must give students work that matches their readiness levels.

In the scene, the teacher addresses her students:

Now, remember, one of the things we talked about is that we all do things differently. For example, Charlie thinks he's fantastic at math, so he took his math dot and put it [in this column] so that we would know he is Fantastic. Sam, however, said, 'Well, I'm not quite so good at math,' and so Sam's dot is over here [at "average"]. (Kiernan, 1997)

When interviewed, the teacher stated that this graphing exercise helps students see, visually, why they may need to work on different projects throughout the year.

Teachers often find that students "quickly come to understand why it's a good idea to differentiate," writes Cindy Strickland in Success with Differentiated Instruction, an ASCD PD Online course (Strickland, 2005). Marion Gilewicz, a teacher from Yellowknife, Northwest Territories, Canada, has been differentiating in her classroom for several years, writes Strickland. She asked some of her students to describe their reactions to what she calls "different-sized learning":

*Students are more successful in school if they are taught in ways that are responsive to their readiness levels, interests, and learning profiles.*

• *Rebecca, age 10—Without different-sized learning, we wouldn't understand so much and our marks would be lower. When we work so it's right for us, our marks grow.*

• *Daniel, age 10—If we had to learn exactly alike, we'd quit being unique. People wouldn't develop their special qualities.*

• *Sonja Lea, age 8—Different-sized learning is when you learn at the right level that is just the right amount of work for you. Not too much and not too little.*

• *Bryan, age 10—Different-sized learning is different people having different activities because they have different learning needs. Imagine if everybody had to do the same thing! Whoa! And, well, thank goodness it's not like that in our classroom. (Strickland, 2005, Lesson 2).*

Children need to understand the rationale for differentiating instruction because teachers need their students' input to do it well, experts note. What's more, by explaining an instructional approach to students, teachers affirm that their students are significant, Carol Ann Tomlinson points out in "Invitations to Learn," (2002). This is key in helping to ensure that students participate fully in the learning program.

Taking time to differentiate instruction—and secure student buy in—does pay off. "There is ample evidence that students are more successful in school and find it more satisfying if they are taught in ways that are responsive to their readiness levels, interests, and learning profiles," Tomlinson writes in "Differentiation of Instruction in the Elementary Grades" (2005, para. 9).

## Respecting Diversity by Individualizing Instruction

Teachers who differentiate instruction often become adept at individualizing instruction and gearing activities to a child's particular learning need. "I try to individualize as much as possible," says Peters, noting that she can't just gear her lessons to the "average 3rd grader" because then she'd lose students on either end of the continuum.

*To boost their understanding of fractions, students in Peters' class measure vegetables using illustrations of worms that represent parts and wholes.*

If students are learning about equivalent fractions, for example, those with a strong understanding of fractions may be asked to work with bigger denominators or improper fractions. These students also could start exploring fraction to decimal or fraction to percentage equivalents. Students who have difficulty understanding fractions, however, may be asked to use manipulatives, such as candy bars or money, to explore the concept, Peters explains. What's imperative, she says, is for all children to feel successful and that they're growing in their knowledge.

Goal setting is another way Peters ensures that her students stretch themselves. "I ask students to tell me, 'What do you need to do and how are you going to get there?'" She and her students meet every quarter, and Peters has found that, through this reflective exercise, students become very realistic about their goals for learning. The information she collects from students is, of course, particularly helpful to Peters as she strives to better tailor her instruction to each student's needs.

Plotycia uses problem-solving strategies to meet students' different needs. She starts by sharing a simple problem with the class, such as:

*How many seats would we need on a bus if we could sit three to a seat and we had twelve students?*

"As a class we discuss how to solve the problem using various strategies," Plotycia explains. "To allow for differentiation, I assign students a partner . . . who demonstrates similar [abilities]. I remind the students that they may solve the problem using any strategy that best suits them."

She ensures that students have access to supplies, including poster paper, markers, macaroni, counters, connecting cubes, ten frames, hundred charts, and calculators. She even has a graphic organizer that consists of a drawing of a bus with empty seats.

"I circulate as the students work," says Plotycia. "If I see a pair struggle, I ask questions that hopefully will guide them into the right direction. If I have a pair that still continues to struggle, I provide them with the organizer and discuss how they might use it with counters to solve the problem. If I observe a pair that completes it quickly and correctly, I direct them to find multiple ways to organize the seating and I caution them to keep their data organized."

When most of the students have completed the problem, Plotycia groups two pairs together and asks the students to discuss their solutions. Did they use the same strategy? Did they get a correction solution? Were any of the solutions the same?

Plotycia then meets again with the whole group for an in-depth discussion. "The students share and discuss strategies used, efficiency, challenges, roadblocks, and their thinking as they worked toward the solution," which ultimately helps all students, she states.

How the classroom is organized can also help teachers individualize instruction, allowing students to determine, with guidance, where their time may be better spent. LeeAnn Cervini, who taught 1st grade for nine years at Terry A. Taylor Elementary School in Spencerport, New York, found that using centers helped her give students choices. "Within a center, I would have choices based on interest or readiness. Students would choose which activity they would want to work on," she explains.

*Using centers helps give students choices.*

The centers helped keep boredom at bay, Cervini recalls. "With young kids, it is very important to keep the flow and momentum going, and you need to take cues from kids. "It's almost like conducting an orchestra," she observes. If students don't find the center activities to be engaging, "behavior issues arise, students become listless, and attention wanders."

Then the teacher has to determine if a student is disengaged because his interests aren't being met or whether the task is either too easy or too difficult. Teachers have to be proactive, she asserts. "You need to know your kids." Cervini, for example, remembers one student who would also lose attention more quickly than the others. So, she placed other activities for him in his folder. He could start a new activity while many of his classmates were still focused on the original task.

## The Learning Styles—Math Connection

In addition to differentiating instruction by interest and readiness, teachers should also consider a student's learning profile, which reflects an understanding of how students learn best, writes Cindy Strickland (2005).

That may be easier said than done when it comes to mathematics instruction, say Harvey F. Silver and Matthew Perini, education consultants with Silver Strong & Associates. In workshops, many math teachers had difficulty determining how they could incorporate an understanding of learning style into their practice. "Math teachers would say, 'Well, that's nice, but how do you do this in mathematics?'" says Silver.

So Perini and Richard Strong, also with Silver Strong & Associates, decided to conduct an in-class experiment: "We said, 'Let's give students some math problems and collect information on how they solved those problems,'" says Perini. They found, perhaps somewhat obviously, that there were "some strong differences in ways children approach mathematics and how they view mathematics." The experiment revealed that there are essentially four types of math students. Teachers must be aware of these types so they can be sure to plan learning activities that honor students' preferred style, says Perini.

Students who want to learn practical information and set procedures are **Mastery** math students. These students like math problems that have been solved before, write Silver and Strong in the introduction to *Styles and Strategies for Teaching Middle School Mathematics* (2003). These students have the most difficulty when math content becomes highly abstract, says Silver in an interview. "If they have a procedure, they're ok, but if they have to discover the strategy they have more difficulty." These students want a math teacher who "models new skills, allows time for practice, and builds in feedback and coaching sessions," write Silver and Strong (p. 13; *see Learning About Money, p. 126*).

**Interpersonal** math students love to learn math through dialogue and group work, says Perini. They like to consider how math helps people and prefer problems that have real-world applica-

## Learning About Money
### *Four Sides of the Same Coin*

Effective teachers use many strategies to draw students into the content. Creating lessons that honor learning styles is one of those strategies.

In this exercise, created by Silver Strong & Associates to meet Kentucky state math standards, students sort objects and compare attributes. The object of choice for this lesson: the four major U.S. coins (this activity could easily be adapted to use any world currency).

**The Scenario:** Money is a difficult concept for young learners because the relationship between coins and their values is arbitrary: there is no inherent reason why a nickel should be five cents or a dime, ten. What's more, the values of various coins can conflict with a young learner's way of thinking. For example, many young learners think that a penny is worth more than a dime because it is bigger. Before students can make the connection between coins and value, they need to be able to discriminate easily between each type. In this activity, students learn to use their sight, touch, growing analytical abilities, and their imaginations to distinguish between the four major U.S. coins. You will need several coins of each type to conduct this activity.

**The Hook:** What kinds of information can you learn when you look at things more closely than usual? Have you ever used a magnifying glass to examine an object and discovered something new about what you were examining? In this activity, we are going to examine coins very closely to see what we can learn about how pennies, nickels, dimes, and quarters are all different from one another.

**Mastery Task, Activity 1:** Using a magnifying glass, describe the characteristics of the following according to this criteria: color, shape, size, words, and pictures:

- penny

- nickel

- dime

- quarter

**Interpersonal Task, Activity 2:** Team up with a friend. Have your friend close his or her eyes.

Your teacher will give you two coins. Can your friend tell you which coin it is without looking?

If you give your friend both coins, can he or she tell which is which?

Now switch places with your friend.

**Understanding Task, Activity 3:** Compare and contrast a penny, a nickel, and a dime. How are they all alike? How is each different from the others?

When you are done with your comparison, you will discuss with the class how you can tell these coins apart.

Now, explain how the quarter is different from the other three you have already compared.

**Self-Expressive Task, Activity 4:** In your journal, write about what you have learned about telling coins apart.

Then, select one coin and write a poem about it.

_____

*Source:* Adapted with permission from Silver Strong & Associates. (2003, March). Thoughtful Education Press. 1-800-962-4432. www.silverstrong.com.

tions. "These are the students who love to talk to their neighbors and experience difficulty when instruction is focused on seat work and independent work," Perini explains. These students "need the teacher to pay attention to them and their struggles with math," he says.

**Understanding** math students are interested in the why of math, explains Perini. They like math problems that ask them to take a position. These students "try to find a pattern and they're always on the lookout for questions or little tricks," Perini says. These students have difficulty when collaboration is part of the lesson, he continues. "These students are most frustrated by group work." The math teacher who challenges students to think and requires them to explain their thinking is most popular with these students, write Silver and Strong (2003; *see p. 126*).

Students who want to use their imagination, that are drawn to projects that allow them to think outside the box, and who tend to visualize problems are **Self-Expressive** math students, says Silver. Self-Expressive students want choice and creativity, he notes, and isn't comfortable in a classroom that emphasizes drill and practice and rote problem solving. What's more, they want teachers who invite creative problem solving into the math classroom, write Silver and Strong (2003).

Awareness of the four types of math students is, of course, a first step. An ideal next step, says Silver, is for teachers to "develop units of instruction that support these learning styles." Unfortunately, he points out, the "overwhelming bias in math instruction is toward one or two styles," adding that the "inability of students to achieve as well as they can in math is as much a style issue as it is a cognitive issue."

## Improving Math Attitudes

Improving achievement in math is systemic, say experts: When students feel safe enough in the classroom to ponder mathematical concepts—and sometimes reveal their misunderstandings—and when students understand and, indeed, embrace the idea that we all learn in different ways and at our own unique pace, math class is no longer a place that some students fear.

"Once I realized that math could be more exciting and fun, I grabbed on to that pretty quickly," says Rose-Piver, the former math-phobic teacher. "I learned that there was more to math than just sitting there and mindlessly doling out a page of math facts." She notes that students with a developed fear or dislike of math came to realize that they would have a good time in her class.

But having a good time didn't mean a lack of rigor, Rose-Piver states. Her students had a good time because they became confident about their ability to do math. "The focus was on perseverance—that with work, understanding would come," she says. Of course, Rose-Piver would offer students many ways to work with a concept in order to help fortify their learning. "I would ask a lot of questions rather than give answers. I had them draw pictures they could understand, and I made sure they knew they could experiment and explore a problem," she says, adding that she hopes

*Students will enjoy math when they become confident about their ability to do math.*

# Building Positive Math Attitudes

### By Laura Varlas

Why do people hate math? Type the phrase "I hate math" into Google, and you'll come up with over 8,000 hits. Try the same with another subject, like English or science. Not even close. When did math get such a bad rap? Or, perhaps more to the point, how did we get such bad attitudes about math? And how are schools trying to change that?

Despite the public's diffidence when it comes to math, Arnie Cutler, executive director for the Minnesota Council of Teachers of Mathematics, believes math is accessible to everyone and that a student's "attitude and work ethic are much more of a factor in determining success." We must adopt classroom practices supporting that positive vision, Cutler says. Actively engaging students in problems, encouraging multiple approaches and solutions to problems, embedding math in the student's world, and using multiple forms of assessment can help every student succeed in math, he adds.

## Positive Math Parenting

Reaching out to parents as much as to students is an important part of the equation, asserts Marc Garneau, president of the British Columbia Association for Mathematics Teachers. "Parents play a very important role," he says. "On one hand, negative attitudes are so easily reinforced by a parent who shares this attitude. On the other hand, even if a parent doesn't like mathematics, there are many things they can do to improve the attitude of their child."

Many schools in British Columbia host "Math Nights for Parents," when parents can experience firsthand the math that their children learn. In addition, Garneau coordinates a Mathematics Playground Kit that schools can sign out to families. Garneau says such initiatives have a "tremendous impact" on enlisting parent support.

*Source:* Adapted from "Taking the Square Route to Positive Math Attitudes," by L. Varlas, 2004, *Curriculum•Technology Quarterly* 13(3), pp. A, D.

the skills her students developed would help them in the years ahead. "I tried to help my students see that even when they leave my room, they can be in control of how they solve problems," Rose-Piver states. She tells students to "take your tool kit, apply the strategies you know, and get into the problem."

"Students will value what the teacher values," maintains Jennifer Buttars, a 2nd grade teacher at Columbia Elementary School in West Jordan, Utah. She says that her students have no doubt that she really enjoys what she does. "I have a blast teaching math, and I tell my students, 'Let me show you how fun math can be.'" And what Buttars fondly hopes is that her enthusiasm will spread. "I hope that my love of math is contagious for most kids."

## Reflections ◆ ◆ ◆

Carol Ann Tomlinson reminds educators that they have a responsibility to invite students to take advantage of the learning opportunities available to them. She adds that, "because students vary, what is inviting will vary as well," (2002, p. 8). That observation invites teachers to look for ways to meet each of their students' unique learning needs. How?

• **Consider the many ways to vary instruction.** Learn all you can about the theory of multiple intelligences, learning styles, differentiated instruction, and so on. Then, take time to put some of your ideas into action and watch how your students respond.

• **Go to the source for help.** Ask your students, their caretakers, and previous teachers about their preferred modes of learning. Then use what you learn to help your students learn better.

5

# Implications for Professional Development

*Life is good for only two things, discovering mathematics and teaching mathematics.*

—*Simeon Poisson*

*The quality of mathematics teaching and learning depends on what teachers do with their students, and what teachers can do with their students depends on their knowledge of mathematics.*

—*RAND* Research Brief, *2003*

Ashley Berk loved math when she was in school; it was a subject she excelled in. When she was a student teacher, however, Berk learned more about how mathematical understanding develops, and she began to question what it meant to be good at mathematics.

Berk, now a 5th grade teacher at Travell Elementary School in Ridgewood, New Jersey, was taking a course designed to help her and her fellow students "unpack" mathematical thinking. She recalls that one night in class, she had solved an assigned problem in about 30 seconds. Berk noticed, however, that many of her classmates were still hard at work. "The teacher came to my desk and asked, 'Are you done? How did you solve this?'" Berk described the procedure she had used (the FOIL method: when multiplying two binomials, multiply the **F**irst terms, then the **O**utside terms, then the **I**nside terms, and finally the **L**ast terms), and her teacher responded with a statement that Berk took to heart:

"Math is a lot bigger than being able to use that process to solve this problem."

That evening, Berk reflected on what they had done in class: they had used manipulatives to physically and visually explore the mathematical concepts, they had explained their reasoning, and they had shared their ideas. The emphasis had been on inquiry, not answers. Berk realized then that a deep understanding of math goes beyond memorizing and applying formulas. "It was a turning point for me as a learner," she recalls. "It made me really think about how kids learn and the way teachers can approach teaching so that you're able to reach all different kinds of learners."

Berk's experience underscores the importance of teachers not only knowing math but also *knowing how to teach* math. Teachers must know how to best help students "strengthen their conceptual understanding of mathematical ideas," she says.

*Teachers must know how to best help students strengthen their conceptual understanding of mathematical ideas.*

## Effective PD: Hard to Measure

Educators agree that student achievement in mathematics will improve only if teachers are knowledgeable about the subject and are comfortable using instructional practices that have been proven effective. But "tracing the causal relationship between professional development and what's enacted in the classroom" is hard to do, says Mark Saul, program director at the National Science Foundation, who also served on the RAND Mathematics Study Panel (*see Chapter 1*).

"The nature of the knowledge required for successful teaching of mathematics is poorly specified," observed authors of the resulting RAND report, *Mathematical Proficiency for All Students: Toward a Strategic Research and Development Program in Mathematics Education* (2003, xvi). The panel, therefore, recommended an extensive research and development program that will help educators gain

• A better understanding of the mathematical knowledge teachers need to be effective in the classroom.

• Improved methods for disseminating useful and usable mathematical knowledge to teachers.

• Valid and reliable measures of the mathematical knowledge teachers have. (RAND Mathematics Study Panel, 2003)

According to the panel, information gathered from a "vigorous and critical research, development, and practice community" would go a long way toward "developing teachers' mathematical knowledge in ways that are directly useful" in helping them help their students attain the skills they need for mathematical thinking and problem solving (2003, p. 78).

Such a research project could investigate a question John Van de Walle has posed: "How do teachers build expertise to be constructivist teachers?" The kind of teaching promoted today is very different than in years past, he notes. Teachers need to pose problems, make sure students understand them, and ensure that they have enough time to work on them, perhaps collaboratively. Teachers should move about the classroom while students work, asking questions, encouraging them to discuss their reasoning with their peers, and suggesting they write about how they solved the problem. Then, says Van de Walle, because students need "an end" to a lesson, teachers can facilitate a debriefing, perhaps in a

*Teaching today is different than in years past. Teachers need to pose problems, make sure students understand them, and provide ample time for students to work on them, perhaps collaboratively.*

whole group setting, and ask students to talk about the processes they used to arrive at their solutions.

To provide this kind of mathematics learning, teachers must "know a whole lot more mathematics—they have to know it deeply," maintains Van de Walle, professor emeritus at Virginia Commonwealth University. Teachers also need to understand how kids learn, he says. For example, after a few months, students will begin to entertain the kinds of questions the teacher initially asks. So teachers must know when it's time to be less directive and more guiding, he says.

Additionally, teachers must learn how to create learning environments that comply with the new "verbs" of the standards-based mathematics classroom, suggests Van de Walle in his textbook, *Elementary and Middle School Mathematics: Teaching Developmentally*, 5th edition (2004). "Children in traditional mathematics classrooms often describe mathematics as 'work' or 'getting answers.' They talk about 'plussing' and 'doing times' (multiplication)," he writes. In contrast, children in constructivist, standards-based classrooms will say they are "exploring," "discovering," "predicting," and "describing" what they've learned. In classrooms where children use these kinds of verbs to describe their activity, "it is virtually impossible for them to be passive observers. They will necessarily be thinking about the mathematical ideas that are involved," writes Van de Walle, (2004, pp. 13, 14).

*Explore, investigate, model, justify—these verbs describe processes used in the service of doing mathematics and science.*

Explore, investigate, model, justify—these verbs describe processes that are "used in the service of doing mathematics and science," observes Thomas P. Carpenter, professor emeritus at University of Wisconsin–Madison. When teachers create learning activities that incorporate these processes, they are really emphasizing learning with understanding, he says. "Mathematics and science becomes easier to learn when it's done this way; it sticks."

And, when students have had a history of such learning experiences, they have a solid foundation on which to build. "Students can then really learn more substantive math and science," Carpenter states.

Both Carpenter and Van de Walle emphasize the importance of professional development. Teachers must learn *how* to provide mathematical learning experiences that require students to explore, investigate, model, and justify. "We can't just create a curriculum and put it into teachers' hands," says Carpenter. Providing sustained and long-term professional development is key to ensuring the curriculum is implemented effectively. "We need professional development that really brings in substantive ideas," Carpenter states. "School must become a place of teacher learning as well as of student learning."

## Effective PD: Some Good Models

One way for schools to provide for teacher learning is by forming collaborations with universities and research centers, suggests Carpenter, who is also the director of the National Center for Improving Student Learning and Achievement in Mathematics and Science (NCISLA), which strives to strengthen teachers' content knowledge and in-class practices. "We work with teachers and help them think about student thinking and help them create lessons for that. There is always interplay between teachers and researchers," says Carpenter.

The NCISLA doesn't provide curriculum. Instead, the center's researchers provide professional development around particular ideas, Carpenter explains. "Our focus is on specific concepts. We provide examples of types of problems, but teachers construct the specific problems that they can adapt with their students," he says. If a teacher needs ideas on how to help students understand how the equal sign is used, for example, the center researchers "acquaint teachers" with the issues related to the concept of equality. "We want to open a window on the kinds of misconceptions kids have," Carpenter states. Then, he and his colleagues help teachers adapt their curriculum. It's a relationship "that treats teachers with respect and not just as consumers of research," he says.

Along with respect comes the recognition that any change takes time; teachers will evolve, states the NCTM's Cathy Seeley. She urges educators to remind teachers that "it will take some time before they become as adept or proficient as they might like." New ways of teaching math require "a strong knowledge of math and a lot of support for teachers to improve their own learning and knowledge," she says.

Educators should also remember that teachers' attitudes about standards-based math evolve too, say reformers. Gail Underwood, a 2nd grade teacher at Grant Elementary School in Columbia, Missouri, recalls that her district's move to standards-based math was a step-by-step process. The math coordinators in the district first piloted *Investigations* (*see Chapter 2*) and decided that the program was a good fit with the district's objectives, says Underwood.

*Effective PD: Have teachers practice using strategies that they will ultimately employ in the classroom.*

Teachers then underwent extensive professional development. To help teachers better understand how an investigation is conducted, the district created adult investigations. "When teachers go down to the 'kid level' of a subject, such as algebra, and do an adult investigation, they see how learners come in [to the content] at different points," Underwood explains. Through the adult investigation, she says, teachers practice using strategies that they can ultimately employ in the classroom to help all their students learn.

# Improving Teacher Practice by Analyzing Student Work

When she was a special education teacher, Amy Colton learned to contemplate her teaching through the efforts of her students. As she reviewed her students' performance on various tasks, she learned to ask herself, "What does this all mean?" If she determined that the students were having problems with content, "I had to question my approach," said Colton. She would then consider new instructional strategies. "I'd think, If I do x then y will happen.'"

Colton urges all teachers to use student work to assess their own effectiveness in the classroom. Student work can be the tools teachers use to "think about teaching in a complex way" and to analyze their practice. When students don't seem to be grasping a concept, Colton advises teachers to then ask, "What does this tell me about the students? What does this tell me about my teaching?"

## Begin by Just Looking

Teachers begin the self-assessment process by identifying what they see in a sample of a student's work, said Colton. In a workshop she conducted, she asked participants to look at a math worksheet completed by a young student. Teachers were not to "interpret" the student's work; they were only "to see." Teachers, said Colton, have to "learn to look" and be descriptive and specific about what is actually on paper or in a display.

In reviewing the worksheet Colton shared, workshop participants found that the student who completed the assignment had inverted the number 5, had declined to answer one question, and had incorrectly assigned place values. Most of the workshop participants failed to point out which questions the student had answered correctly, Colton observed, noting that teachers must also pay attention to what a student "gets right," because correct answers help teachers determine what teaching strategies work.

Once teachers have identified what they see, they can then interpret what the student performance means, said Colton. In this interpretation stage, teachers ask, "What does this paper tell me?"

As teachers analyzed the worksheet Colton shared, they realized that they first had to know more about the student if the analysis was to be valid. They needed answers to such questions as: What grade is the child in? Where does the topic for this worksheet fall in the sequence of math lessons? Has the student just been introduced to place value? Has this student had a lot of practice with this concept? Is a worksheet the best way for this student to demonstrate his understanding?

The questions teachers ask about student work are far more helpful in improving teaching and learning than the final score marked on the top of the page, said Colton. "Teachers learn to ask, 'Where did I miss the boat?' 'Where are the gaps and how should my instruction help to fill those gaps?'" Colton said.

## Mapping an Instructional Course

The answers to the questions teachers pose about a student's work can also be used to help teachers identify learning objectives for the student.

A teacher may determine, for example, that the student who completed the math worksheet needs to better understand place value. With this learning objective identified, the teacher can then list some instructional approaches that will help the student reach that goal. Teachers should be careful,

Colton advised, to explain why they think certain approaches will work. How might peer instruction help this student? Is one-on-one coaching with the teacher a better option, and if so, why?

As teachers implement the instructional approaches, a new cycle of evaluation begins. Teachers must observe the results, analyze and interpret the effect, and decide what to do next.

Throughout the process, teachers need to ask "How is it going?" and "How do I know?" Teachers begin to "look at the lesson from different perspectives," Colton said. Teachers learn from their experiences and realize that if an instructional approach doesn't work, "it's not because the idea is bad, but because it's not working with a current group of students."

What's more, said Colton, the process of using student work to analyze instructional effectiveness has a profound impact on teachers' self-efficacy. "When teachers go through this process, they feel more empowered," she stated. Teachers begin to realize that they can find a way to make sure their students "get it."

*Source:* From "Learning to Look: Analyzing Student Work to Improve Teacher Practice," by K. Checkley, 2000, *Classroom Leadership* 3(5). Retrieved June 28, 2005, from www.ascd.org

Soon after the professional development effort was underway, the math coordinators "took the textbooks out of our building," says Underwood. Some teachers remained resistant—until, that is, students' performance on statewide and national assessments "showed that we were heading in the right direction." Now, even the once-unenthusiastic teachers are beginning to appreciate the program, she states.

Grant Elementary School's experience with mathematics reform illustrates Seeley's observation that schools and teachers who are successful with change rethink the curriculum with an eye on their own long-term educational objectives. She points to a teacher enhancement project in West Virginia as a model for others. In the five years the project was underway, "they did exactly what the NCTM standards had suggested they do." Educators envisioned what their mathematics classes could be, allowed districts to tailor the vision to meet their specific needs, identified curricula packages (an overwhelming majority of counties—90 percent—chose curriculum endorsed by the National Science Foundation), and then trained the teachers. "They took the vision of the NCTM standards, translated it through state standards, and found curriculum materials to support that vision," says Seeley.

## Effective PD: Worth the Effort

These professional development efforts come none too soon, says Saul. In a recent workshop he conducted, Saul found that many teachers didn't see how what they taught laid the foundation for later learning. Teachers "can't just *assume* that the mathematics knowledge will be served" by what they teach, Saul states. Instead, teachers should *know* it. They should know *how* the concepts they teach are directly tied to what comes later, he affirms.

Underwood agrees. "When I came into teaching 14 years ago, I didn't understand my students' thinking; I didn't understand the math. Now, I have a deep understanding of 2nd grade mathematics and, with more learning and mentoring, I'll understand all elementary-level mathematics," she says. "I see myself as a poster child for good professional development."

The more she learns, the more Underwood sees herself as a teacher leader "there to support people as they develop." Underwood anticipates that she and her colleagues will meet regularly to ensure they deliver a sound curriculum. Their next challenge: to tackle the depth versus breadth issue. It's a national problem, says Underwood. "We don't spend enough time really developing concepts." What would happen, she wonders, "if we had good professional development, if teachers were allowed to stay in grade levels for a period of time to really know content, and if we deepened curriculum?" With an emphasis on depth, Underwood asserts that teachers could scan the K–12 mathematics learning plan and determine at each level what they needed to know in order to teach.

"What do teachers really need to know in order to teach? That's an interesting question," says Leanne Luttrell, who teaches 4th and 5th grade gifted students at Sycamore Elementary School in Sugar Hill, Georgia. Undergraduate students "have so many methods classes," but they really need "to be immersed in the content," says Luttrell. She remembers that, after teaching a lesson on dividing fractions, she was surprised when a colleague asked her: "How did you know how that would work? How did you think of that idea?" Teachers, maintains Luttrell, should have this math content knowledge before they get into a classroom.

Beth Peters had a similar experience. The 3rd grade teacher at Village East Elementary School, in Aurora, Colorado, watched as her student teacher worked with a student on an addition problem. When asked to add 82 and 88, the child answered "1610," says Peters. The child had just been introduced to place value and double-digit addition, so what she did made some sense—but the student teacher didn't recognize the opportunity to clarify a concept.

So, Peters says she stepped in and, after congratulating the student for knowing that she must add the ones together and the 10s together, asked the student if the answer was reasonable. "Does it really make sense that if you add 80 and 80 that you would have such a large number?" Peters asked. In asking, Peters helped build the knowledge of two people at once. The student was taught to reflect on what she knew about numbers to evaluate her response and the student teacher learned how to pose questions that would guide the student down the right path. When adults share strategies, says Peters, it's powerful.

*Effective PD: Teachers should share successful strategies.*

## Effective PD: Lesson Study

Sharing strategies and having adult conversations about learning and teaching are all part of a practice called *lesson study*.

The term comes from the Japanese word *jugyokenkyuu*, which describes the professional development model that Japanese teachers have perfected (Teachers College, 2002). "During lesson study, a group of teachers researches and writes a lesson plan on a particular theme," writes Ellen R. Delisio in "Lesson Study: Practical Professional Development" (2004). The plan also includes the teachers' expectations for the lesson: How will it help students understand a certain concept better?

"Once the lesson is completed, one teacher from the group volunteers to teach it to his or her class, and the other teachers are given release time to observe the implementation of the lesson and note if and how it met expectations," Delisio writes. Teachers then meet again, "review notes, and decide what revisions are needed," she explains (2004, para. 6).

"The Japanese do a mile deep and an inch wide," says Linda Figgins, a 6th grade teacher at McKinley Elementary in Elgin, Illinois. She believes that lesson study is what helps Japanese teachers perfect their lessons, because they're always "looking at what the lesson is doing for the children." Lesson study, she says, "is how they help their teachers develop their questioning techniques."

Figgins, who has watched videotapes of 8th grade mathematics teachers from several countries, including Japan (*see Let's Go to the Video Tape, p. 134*) used the lesson study approach with the college students she teaches. "I had teachers team up with different grade levels to study the lesson I submitted for the presidential awards," Figgins explains. Each of her undergraduate education students taught the lesson for their grade level. "It was powerful," Figgins states. "The emphasis was on the concept of the lesson rather than on the level of the child." The questions may change per grade level, and grade level determines how far a teacher can take the lesson, Figgins notes, but the concept stays the same.

Jennifer Buttars likes to extend the idea of lesson study into something she and her colleagues call *practice* study. The 2nd grade teacher at Columbia Elementary School in West Jordan, Utah, says that "when we did lesson study, we'd talk beforehand about goals and what we were looking for." During the following debrief, "we'd discuss our observations and concerns" about the lesson.

But Buttars felt the study could also be used to gauge the effectiveness of teaching, not just of the lesson. So she created a framework that would allow teachers to, among other things,

# Let's Go to the Video Tape

*How does mathematics instruction differ from country to country?*

*What do these international comparisons tell us about how to improve mathematics achievement?*

Education professors James W. Stigler and James Hiebert have spent 10 years researching the answers to these questions by studying videotapes of the instruction provided by 8th grade mathematics teachers in different countries. "These teachers are not necessarily experienced or effective. They are ordinary teachers teaching lessons that they routinely teach," write Stigler and Hiebert in "Improving Mathematics Teaching" (2004, p. 12).

Stigler and Hiebert decided to review "ordinary" lessons because "these lessons together represent what average teaching looks like in different countries." What's more, "studying a national sample of classroom lessons can help us discover whether policy initiatives have influenced classroom practice." Also, write the authors, "studying lessons from different cultures gives researchers and teachers the opportunity to discover alternative ideas about how we can teach mathematics."

The first video study, conducted by the Third International Mathematics and Science Survey (TIMSS, now Trends in International Mathematics and Science Study), was done in 1995 and examined national samples of 8th grade mathematics lessons from three countries: Germany, Japan, and the United States. The second TIMSS video study, conducted in 1999, expanded on the first study. In addition to the United

States, Australia, the Czech Republic, Hong Kong, Japan, the Netherlands, and Switzerland were included.

"The design of the 1999 video study was simple," write Stigler and Hiebert. "We selected a random sample of 100 8th grade mathematics classrooms from each country and videotaped them at some point during the school year. We digitized, transcribed, and translated the tapes into English, after which an international team of researchers analyzed them." According to Stigler and Hiebert, the video study revealed that:

**Effective teaching takes many forms.** The videotapes from each country revealed that many of the teaching methods that are hotly debated in the United States are used to varying degrees by the six higher-achieving countries. For example, the Netherlands uses calculators and real-world problem scenarios quite frequently. Japan does neither. Yet both countries have high levels of student achievement.

**Implementation is important.** What do the higher-achieving countries have in common? ask Stigler and Hiebert. "The way in which teachers and students work on problems as the lesson unfolds," they write. In those countries in which students perform well in mathematics, most teachers try to help students make connections with the content. In the United States, teachers turned most of the problems into procedural exercises. Indeed, U.S. 8th graders spend most of their time in mathematics classrooms practicing procedures. They rarely spend time engaged in the serious study of mathematical concepts.

**Teaching can be improved by focusing on the details of teaching, not teachers.** "Most current efforts to improve the quality of teaching focus on the teacher: how the profession can recruit more qualified teachers and how we can remedy deficiencies in the knowledge of current teachers," write Stigler and Hiebert. The focus should instead be on improving teaching, on "the methods that teachers use in the classroom."

Educators should remember that the methods teacher choose to use are usually culture based, Stigler and Hiebert continue. In their study, for example, even with standards-based materials that foster inquiry, many teachers in the United States were still using a traditional approach to math instruction.

That can only change if teachers see how to improve their instruction, suggest the authors. In implementing "making connections problems," for example, some teachers will come up against a formidable challenge: They might never have seen what it looks like to implement these problems effectively. "Teachers need access to examples, such as those collected in the TIMSS video studies. They need to decide how they can integrate these examples into their own practice. They need to analyze what happens when they try something new in their own teaching: Does it help students achieve the learning goals?" Teachers should then record what they learn and share that knowledge with their colleagues, recommend Stigler and Hiebert.

"Teachers have a central role to play in building a useful knowledge base for the profession," write the authors. "Enabling teachers to learn about teaching practices in other countries and to reflect on the implications of those practices holds great promise for improving the mathematics instruction provided to all students."

*Source:* Adapted from "Improving Mathematics Teaching," by J. W. Stigler and J. Hiebert, 2004, *Educational Leadership* 61(5), pp. 12–17.

assess whether their instruction helped students attain a conceptual understanding of the topic. "It was more a *practice* study," she states.

Buttars and her colleagues hope to expand the use of practice study, involving teachers from a range of grade levels—including secondary math. "It will be fascinating to see [how concepts] are addressed at different grade levels," says Buttars.

## Effective PD: Finding Time

Any kind of professional development effort, whether it's partnering with researchers at a university or engaging in lesson study, takes time—time that is hard to find in already-filled days, many educators assert.

"In order to teach math in this way, you're really challenging the way you learned math," says Berk. And, she points out, "although many adults are in book clubs on their own, not so many get together in math clubs to solve problems together." Some daily activities may strengthen a person's math *skills* to a certain extent, Berk states. "But I don't know if those activities strengthen a *conceptual* understanding of math." So, teachers must make time to go back and revisit concepts that they covered so long ago, she says.

Should teachers, however, be expected to attend professional development sessions on their own time, Underwood asks. "In the business world, if you have a meeting from 9 to 10, you're paid for it. As a teacher who has a passion for learning and the art of teaching, I use a lot of my own time," she says. Indeed, Underwood likes the time she spends in school to be well spent. "There seem to be a lot of meetings that have nothing to do with instruction," she observes.

*Effective PD: Make a commitment to continuous learning.*

Such challenges aside, most teachers will find time to deepen their own understanding of math content. Teachers have to keep themselves fresh, says Mary Short, a 2nd grade teacher at Long Neck Elementary School in Millsboro, Delaware. "I read professional articles on different things I should keep up on," she notes. "You just have to make yourself available. You have to make a commitment to continuous learning."

Luttrell agrees. "I take workshops and go to mathematics conferences every year," she says. "Our goal is for our students to be lifelong learners. We should model what that looks like."

## Reflections ◆ ◆ ◆

*If teachers simply teach lessons, one after another, and never take time to ask themselves whether those lessons were effective or what they could have done differently, the learning process of teaching is hindered.*

—The Teacher Series: Teacher as Reflector Learner

This chapter has been about teachers learning to improve instruction. As the previous quote suggests, reflection is critical to growth—for any learner of any age.

• **Learn to ask, What happened? Why did it happen?** What might it mean? What are the implications for my practice? According to Linda Lambert, an ASCD author who contributed her expertise to *The Teacher Series*, when teachers reflect on those questions, they begin to use the reflective process as a way to say, 'Well, I interacted with the students in that way, what happened?'"

• **Reach out to colleagues,** Lambert advises. Ask them, What do you think about . . . ? And, Are you doing anything like this? Tell them, When I tried that, this is how it went. . .

• **Engage in such things as dialogue, reflective writing, and networking,** Lambert says. "Being part of an inquiry-based practice in the school [is] actually critical because then growth spirals," she maintains. "And once we get really under-way, there's no stopping teachers because they are lifelong learners."

# Looking Forward

*There are three kinds of people in this world: those who can count and those who cannot.*

—*Anonymous*

When Linda Figgins isn't teaching her 6th grade students at McKinley Elementary School in Eglin, Illinois, she can be found at Northern Illinois University working with adults who are seeking provisional certification, as well as those earning master's degrees and teaching certificates. She finds it very rewarding to think she's serving many children by reaching their teachers. Figgins feels especially satisfied when she helps math-phobic adults realize that they can, indeed, comprehend concepts that once seemed utterly beyond their grasp.

She begins by asking her students to write their math autobiographies. How would they describe their math learning experiences? Figgins recalls that one young man drew a zero to represent himself. Teachers, the young man said, thought he was "retarded in math" because he couldn't immediately use an algorithm to solve equations. This same young man, however, was able to use manipulatives to solve the toughest of equations, reaching a conclusion more quickly than even those who were considered "successful" with math.

A number of the teachers interviewed for this book might have written similar biographies. "I was math phobic and really didn't want to take math courses," recalls Francine Plotycia, the 2nd grade teacher from Abingdon Elementary School in Maryland. "I took statistics and graduate-level algebra and geometry—it was all pretty tough. I just didn't understand what the professor was doing." Plotycia says she now enjoys the math she and her students work on "because it makes sense."

Beth Peters, the 3rd grade teacher at Village East Elementary School in Aurora, Colorado, will often tell her students that "math wasn't hard for me, but it wasn't easy, either." She also recognizes that encouragement works hand-in-hand with perseverance. So Peters tries to ensure that every child feels successful in math, no matter how they struggle.

Valerie Rose-Piver's struggles with school mathematics are described in Chapter 4. Fortunately, she participated in good professional development and found a new enthusiasm for the subject. "I always thought my program was pretty boring," Rose-Piver says. "Now I know that math can be exciting and fun—there's more to math than just sitting there and mindlessly doling out page after page of math facts."

Tomorrow's teachers will share very different math stories if mathematics reformers have their way. In future autobiographies, students may still write that they were required to hone basic arithmetic skills and solve equations, says NCTM's Cathy Seeley. But tomorrow's teachers will also have learned that "computation is only part of a balanced math program."

Tomorrow's teachers, she notes, will have problem-solving skills and the ability to reason and to explain that reasoning to others. Tomorrow's teachers will have a deeper understanding of the concepts—they'll know what the numbers and operations mean, Seeley states.

Ultimately, of course, tomorrow's teachers will then be prepared to bring tomorrow's students to a new level of competency in math.

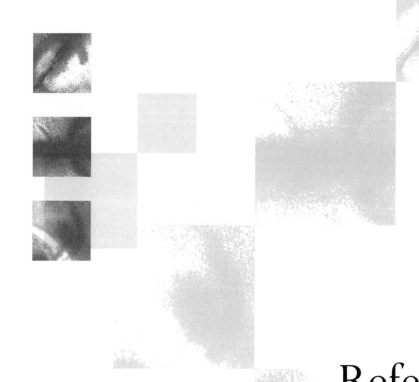

# References

# Introduction

Adelman, C. (1999). *Answers in the tool box: Academic intensity, attendance patterns, and bachelor's degree attainment*. Washington, DC: U.S. Department of Education.

Armstrong, T. (2003). *Multiple intelligences of reading and writing: Making the words come alive*. Alexandria, VA: Association for Supervision and Curriculum Development.

Association for Supervision Curriculum Development. (December 2004/ January 2005). Ranking math and science students internationally. *Ed Policy Update 3*(12). Retrieved October 21, 2005, from www.ascd.org

Bohan, J. (2002). *Mathematics: A chapter of the curriculum handbook*. Alexandria, VA: Association for Supervision and Curriculum Development.

Carnevale, A., & Desrochers, D. (2002). Connecting education standards and employment: Course-taking patterns of young workers. American Diploma Project: Workplace Study. Retrieved November 2, 2005, from www.achieve.org/dstore.nsf/Lookup/ADP_Workplace_12-9-02/$file /ADP_Workplace_12-9-02.pdf

Goldsmith, L. T., & Kantrov, I. (2001). *Guiding curriculum decisions for middle-grades mathematics*. Portsmouth, NH: Heinemann.

Holloway, J. H. (2004). Research link: Closing the achievement gap in math. *Educational Leadership 61*(5), 84–86.

Kilpatrick, J., & Swafford, J. (Eds.). (2002). *Helping children learn mathematics*. Washington, DC: National Academy Press. Retrieved October 17, 2005, from www.nap.edu/books/0309084318/html

Mirra, A. J. (2003). *Administrator's guide: How to support and improve mathematics education in your school.* Reston, VA: National Council of Teachers of Mathematics.

Posamentier, A. S. (2004). Marvelous math! *Educational Leadership, 61*(5), 44–49.

RAND Mathematics Study Panel. (2003). *Mathematical proficiency for all students: Toward a strategic research and development program in mathematics education.* Santa Monica, CA: RAND.

Rose, H., & Betts, J. R. (2001). *Math matters: The links between high school curriculum, college graduation, and earnings.* San Francisco: Public Policy Institute of California.

Silver, H. F., & Strong, R. W. (2003). Building the 21st century math classroom: An introduction. In E. Thomas, *Styles and strategies for teaching middle school mathmatics* (pp. 5–15). Ho Ho Kus, NJ: Thoughtful Education Press.

# Chapter 1

Battista, M. T. (2001). Research and reform in mathematics education. *The great curriculum debate: How should we teach reading and math?* Washington, DC: The Brookings Institution.

Carpenter, P. T., & Romberg, T. A. (2004). *Powerful practices in mathematics and science.* Madison, WI: The Board of Regents, University of Wisconsin System. (Available from Learning Point Associates online at mscproducts@contact.learningpt.org)

Checkley, K. (2001). Algebra and activism: Removing the shackles of low expectations—A conversation with Robert P. Moses. *Educational Leadership 59*(2), 6–11.

Goldsby, D. S., & Cozza, B. (2002). Writing samples to understand mathematical thinking. *Mathematics Teaching in the Middle School, 7*(9), 517.

NCTM, Marco Polo, & The MCI Foundation. (2005). Data does it—Planning a trip: Unit review. Illuminations. Reston, VA: NCTM. Retrieved October 24, 2005, from http://illuminations.nctm.org/index_o.aspx?id=115

RAND Mathematics Study Panel. (2003). *Mathematical proficiency for all students: Toward a strategic research and development program in mathematics education.* Santa Monica, CA: RAND.

Seeley, C. (2005, March 16). "Pushing Algebra Down" [online chat transcript]. Reston, VA: NCTM. Retrieved October 24, 2005, from www.nctm.org/news/chat_031605.htm

Seeley, C. (2004). *A journey in algebraic thinking.* Retrieved May 16, 2005, from www.nctm.org/news/president/2004_09president.htm

Sjoberg, C. A., Slavit, D., & Coon, T. (2004). Improving writing prompts to improve student reflection. *Mathematics Teaching in the Middle School, 9*(9), 490.

## Chapter 2

Beane, J. A. (1995). *Toward a coherent curriculum (1995 ASCD Yearbook).* Alexandria, VA: Association for Supervision and Curriculum Development.

Bohan, J. (2002). *Mathematics: A chapter of the curriculum handbook.* Alexandria, VA: Association for Supervision and Curriculum Development.

Checkley, K. (2002). *Crafting Curriculum* [online course]. Retrieved October 18, 2005, from http://pdonline.ascd.org

Goldsmith, L. T., & Kantrov, I. (2001). *Guiding curriculum decisions for middle-grades mathematics.* Portsmouth, NH: Heinemann.

The K–12 Mathematics Curriculum Center. (2005). *Curriculum Summaries* (8th ed.). Newton, MA: Education Development Center. Retrieved October 18, 2005, from www2.edc.org/mcc/curricula.asp

Reys, B. J., Reys, R. E., & Chávez, O. (2004). Mathematics textbooks matter. *Educational Leadership 61*(5), 64–65.

Santilli, M. (2004). Elementary math software that makes kids think. *Curriculum•Technology Quarterly 13*(3), 7–8.

Schmidt, W. (2004). A vision for mathematics. *Educational Leadership 61*(5), 6–11.

TERC. (n.d.). Two grade 5 activities from *Containers and Cubes*. Retrieved October 24, 2005, from http://investigations.terc.edu/curr/activity5.cfm

Tile Designs: Second Grade Sample Activity. (2005). *Math Trailblazers*. Dubuque, IA: Kendall/Hunt Publishing.

Toombs, W., & Tierney, W. (1993). Curriculum definitions and reference points. *Journal of Curriculum and Supervision, 8*(3), 175–195.

Tyler, R. W. (1949). *Basic principles of curriculum and instruction*. Chicago: University of Chicago Press.

Varlas, L. (2004). Viewpoint. *Curriculum•Technology Quarterly 13*(3), B–C.

Wiggins, G., & McTighe, J. (2005). *Understanding by design, expanded 2nd edition*. Alexandria, VA: Association for Supervision and Curriculum Development.

University of Chicago Mathematics Project. (2003). 1.2 Line Plots. Retrieved October 24, 2005, from http://everydaymath.uchicago.edu/samplelessons/6th/index.html

Witt, P. (Ed). (2005). What the United States can learn from Singapore's world-class mathematics system (and what Singapore can learn from the United States): An exploratory study. Washington, DC: American Institutes for Research. Retrieved October 24, 2005, from www.air.org/news/documents/Singapore%20Report%20(Bookmark%20Version).pdf

## Chapter 3

Association for Supervision and Curriculum Development. (2005). *What we believe: Positions of the Association for Supervision and Curriculum Development*. Retrieved October 18, 2005, from www.ascd.org/ASCD/pdf/newsandissues/What%20We%20Believe/WhatWeBelieve.pdf

D'Arcangelo, M. (Producer). (2001). *The brain and mathematics: Making number sense* [Video program]. Alexandria: VA: Association for Supervision and Curriculum Development.

Clement, L., & Bernhard, J. (2005). A problem-solving alternative to using key words. *Mathematics Teaching in the Middle School, 10*(7), 360–364.

Clooney, B. (1985). *Miss Rumphius*. New York: Puffin Books.

Fitzpatrick, K. (2002). *Leadership and accountability: Maximizing research-based practices and data-driven decision making for school improvement.* From a presentation given at the 2002 ASCD Teaching and Learning Conference [audio program]. Alexandria, VA: Association for Supervision and Curriculum Development.

Hansford, C. (2004). Using math to teach thinking. *Classroom Leadership, 7*(6), 2, 8.

Herrera, T. (2001). An interview with Marilyn Burns: Meeting the standards—Don't try to do it all by yourself. *ENC Focus 8*(2), 16–19.

Hunter, M. (1992). *How to change to a nongraded school.* Alexandria, VA: Association for Supervision and Curriculum Development.

McDonald, B. (2004). Self-assessment for student success. *Classroom Leadership, 8*(1), 4–5.

NCTM. (2005). Overview of principles and standards for school mathematics. Retrieved December 30, 2005, from www.nctm.org/standards

Nuckolls, B. (1998). *Pólya's how to solve it.* Retrieved June 15, 2005, from www.math.grin.edu/~rebelsky/ProblemSolving/Essays/polya.html

Pólya, G. (1985). *How to solve it* (2nd edition, copyright renewed). Princeton, NJ: Princeton University Press

Sanchez, W. B., & Ice, N. F. (2005). Strike a balance in assessment. *News Bulletin May/June* [online article]. Reston, VA: NCTM. Retrieved October 25, 2005, from www.nctm.org/news/assessment/2005_05nb.htm

The Value of Formatiave Assessment. (1999). *FairTest Examiner.* Retrieved October 12, 2005, from www.fairtest.org/examarts/winter99/k-forma3.html

Van Hiele, P. M. (1999). Developing geometric thinking through activities that begin with play. *Teaching Children Mathmatics 5*(6), 310–316.

Van de Walle, J. (2004). *Elementary and middle school mathematics: Teaching developmentally* (5th ed.). Boston: Allyn and Bacon.

Zimmer, J., Dowshen, A., & Ebersole, D. (2004). *IMAGES: A resource guide for improving measurement and geometry in elementary schools.* Philadelphia, PA: Research for Better Schools.

## Chapter 4

Kiernan, L. (Producer). (1997). Differentiating instruction: Instruction and management strategies, tape 2 [video program]. Alexandria, VA: Association for Supervision and Curriculum Development.

Seeley, C. (2005, August 31). Untapped Potential [online chat transcript]. Reston, VA: NCTM. Retrieved October 26, 2005, from www.nctm.org/news/chat_083105.htm

Silver Strong & Associates. (2003). *Middle school mathematics: The hook.* Ho Ho Kus, NJ: Thoughtful Education Press.

Silver, H. F., & Strong, R. W. (2003). Building the 21st century math classroom: An introduction. In E. Thomas, *Styles and strategies for teaching middle school mathematics,* (pp. 5–15). Ho Ho Kus, NJ: Thoughtful Education Press.

Strickland, C. (2005). *Success with Differentiation* [online course]. Alexandria, VA: Association for Supervision and Curriculum Development.

Tomlinson, C. A. (2002). Invitations to learn. *Educational Leadership, 60*(1), 6–10.

Tomlinson, C. A. (2005). Differentiation of instruction in the elementary grades [ERIC online article]. Retrieved October 18, 2005, from www.ericdigests.org/2001-2/elementary.html

Varlas, L. (2004). Taking the square route to positive math attitudes. *Curriculum•Technology Quarterly, 13*(3), A, D.

Willis, S., & Mann, L. (2000, Winter). Differentiating instruction: Finding manageable ways to meet individual needs. *Curriculum Update*, pp. 1–3, 6, 7.

# Chapter 5

Checkley, K. (2000). Learning to look: Analyzing student work to improve teacher practice. *Classroom Leadership* 3(5). Retrieved June 28, 2005, from www.ascd.org

Delisio, E. (2004). Lesson Study: Practical Professional Development. *Education World* [online article]. Retrieved October 25, 2005, from www.education-world.com/a_admin/admin/admin382.shtml

RAND Mathematics Study Panel. (2003). *Mathematical proficiency for all students: Toward a strategic research and development program in mathematics education.* Santa Monica, CA: RAND.

Stigler, J. W., & Hiebert, J. (2004). Improving mathematics teaching. *Educational Leadership, 6*(5), 12–17.

Teachers College. (2002, Spring/Summer). What is Lesson Study? [online course]. Retrieved October 25, 2005, from www.tc.edu/lessonstudy/lessonstudy.html

Van de Walle, J. (2004). *Elementary and middle school mathematics: Teaching developmentally* (5th ed.). Boston: Allyn and Bacon.

# Index

QA135.6/.C525/2006
The essentials of mathematics K-6 : effective
curriculum, instruction, and assessment / Kathy
Checkley.